Blinded by **Fear**

Also from Phoenesse

GET A BETTER BOAT
Trustworthy Teachings
for Difficult Times

AFTER THE EGO
Insights From the Pathwork® Guide
on How to Wake Up

WALKER
A Memoir

LIVING LIGHT
On Seeking and Finding True Faith

WORD FOR WORD
An Intimate Exchange Between a Couple of Kindred Souls
By Jill Loree and Scott Wisler

The *Real. Clear.* series offers a fresh approach to timeless spiritual teachings, conveying profound ideas by way of easier-to-read language. It's the Pathwork Guide's wisdom in Jill Loree's words.

HOLY MOLY
The Story of Duality, Darkness and a Daring Rescue

FINDING GOLD
The Search for Our Own Precious Self

BIBLE ME THIS
Releasing the Riddles of Holy Scripture

THE PULL
Relationships & Their Spiritual Significance

PEARLS
A Mind-Opening Collection of 17 Fresh Spiritual Teachings

GEMS
A Multifaceted Collection of 16 Clear Spiritual Teachings

BONES
A Building-Block Collection of 19 Fundamental Spiritual Teachings

NUTSHELLS
Snippets from *Pearls*, *Gems* and *Bones*

SPIRITUAL LAWS
Hard & Fast Logic for Forging Ahead

The *Self. Care.* How-to-Heal series offers a bird's-eye view of the Pathwork Guide's teachings and shows us how to apply them in working with others and ourselves.

SPILLING THE SCRIPT
A Concise Guide to Self-Knowing

HEALING THE HURT
How to Help Using Spiritual Guidance

DOING THE WORK
Healing Our Body, Mind & Spirit by Getting to Know the Self

By Jill Loree with Scott Wisler

www.phoenesse.com

The Guide Speaks website delivers spiritual truths by way of thousands of questions posed to the Guide and answered with candor and insight.

THE GUIDE SPEAKS
The Complete Q&A Collection

By Eva Pierrakos with Jill Loree

KEYWORDS
Answers to Key Questions
Asked of the Pathwork® Guide

By Eva Pierrakos with Jill Loree

www.theguidespeaks.com

Blinded by **Fear**

Insights From the Pathwork® Guide
on How to Face Our Fears

By Jill Loree

Published by Phoenesse LLC
www.phoenesse.com

ISBN: 9781732735811

Litany Against Fear

I must not fear.

Fear is the mind-killer.

Fear is the little-death that brings total obliteration.

I will face my fear.

I will permit it to pass over me and through me.

And when it has gone past I will turn the inner eye to see its path.

Where the fear has gone there will be nothing.

Only I will remain.

—An incantation used by the Bene Gesserit throughout the science-fiction series *Dune*, written by Frank Herbert, to focus their minds and calm themselves in times of peril.

Preface

Did you ever look out the window of a plane and see a solid carpet of clouds? They appear to go on forever, and they look so real. Indeed, they are real, yet they are not something we can walk on. And of course we know this. So when it comes to clouds, it's not hard to realize that all is not as it appears.

But then, did you ever have a fear arise in you that you just couldn't shake. You knew it wasn't real—after all, fear is an illusion, right?—but still. If we want to come out from under our fears, we'll need to sort through them and see what they're made of. We'll need to learn about these fantastic illusions so the next time we see one, we won't fall so easily under its spell.

So let's jump in. It's time to see, for real, what's hiding behind our fears.

–Jill Loree
Founder of Phoenesse

Contents

BLINDED BY FEAR

Chapter 1

The Mother of All Fears: Fear of Self

The key to becoming who we truly are is this: We must overcome our fear of ourselves. This is the fundamental prerequisite for being all that we can be. In fact, in the final analysis, every kind of fear amounts to a fear of the self. For if we had no fear of our innermost selves, we couldn't possibly fear anything in life. We wouldn't even fear death.

But when we start to make our way along a path of self-confrontation, we don't know that what we really fear is what lurks in our own unplumbed depths. And so it is that we so often project this very real fear of self onto all kinds of other miscellaneous fears. Then we deny we have those fears, and we set about covering them up.

Until one day we wake up and realize we have some enormous fear of some particular aspect of life upon which this tsunami of fear of our self has landed. Or maybe we just end up fearing life itself and so endeavor to avoid living it altogether. We do this in the same way we avoid knowing the self, to whatever extent it's feared.

To go one further, we'll sometimes project our fear of life onto the fear of death, since really life and death are two sides of the same coin. So actually, if we fear one we're going to also fear the other. Fear of life and death, then, are a package deal.

Only when our search for self-knowing has gained a little traction do we become aware that what we're really most afraid of is ourselves. We can recognize this by the backpedaling we do when it comes to seeing our part in our problems; when we resist, in all the more or less obvious ways we do so; when we won't face our terror of letting go of our defenses, which would allow us to experience our natural feelings.

But the degree of our guardedness won't be clear to us to begin with, because our guards have become second nature to us. We don't even realize at this point that they're unnatural and that life could be oh-so-very-different if we would just let them go. In truth, our inability to relax and let ourselves be guided by involuntary forces is a key sign of how much we distrust ourselves.

And exactly why do we hold back from allowing natural soul movements to guide us? Because we're afraid of them, that's why. We're afraid of where they will take us. To simply become aware of this fear is to take a giant leap in the right direction, heading toward self-liberation, toward freedom from fear. For if we're not aware of our fear of our self, it can't be overcome.

The Real Self

Our Real Self cannot be manipulated into freedom; it can't be forced or coerced into showing up and behaving well. Our Real Self can only manifest as a spontaneous expression. So if we're afraid to let go, well then, we'll stay locked in a prison of our own making.

What does it look like when our Real Self acts spontaneously? We intuitively know things that arise from within, not by way of an outer learning process. Genuine artists and clever scientists alike bring new creations into the world through this process, but for this to happen they must not fear their inner selves. Too often, they unknowingly block what wants to come bubbling to life.

When we fear what will happen if we don't conform to our social environment, we're experiencing yet another twist on the theme of Fear of Self. For it could happen that our true inner reality is at odds with what's happening in our world; our inner values might be different from the values handed down to us. When that's the case, our work is to refuse ready-made values, and we can only do that if we don't fear what organically arises from inside. Whether they're right or wrong, outer values will feel like shackles if we don't choose them freely.

One of the biggest kickers about our fear of self is the way it dovetails with fear of pleasure. For we humans are pleasure-making machines, capable of experiencing intense joy. That said, a whole lot of people don't enjoy any positive pleasure at all. And that's a real shame, because every human alive comes factory-installed with the ability to surrender fully to the life force and all its tantalizing pleasure currents.

If we're truly healthy and functioning as we're meant to, we will spontaneously express this powerful force as it comes rolling through us. We won't fear it and therefore we won't reject it. It will light us up like a Christmas tree, enlivening us with gorgeous energy, tremendous strength and deep delight.

But for those of us who remain guarded and defended, who are constantly keeping themselves in check out of fear of letting go, these forces can't shine. When we numb ourselves by deadening our feelings, we effectively—no surprise—become dead. This lack of aliveness, or state of disconnectedness, is rampant throughout our world, but no more so today than in previous eras. We could call it self-alienation, and in its wake flows a sense of meaninglessness and emptiness. All because our overly watchful, willful ego won't let go.

Sure, the average Joe and Joanne experience some level of aliveness, at least sometimes. But it's a pittance compared to what's possible. We can't even imagine how much better things could be. Too often we label such aliveness as "unrealistic," or maybe even think our longing for a different way of life is an illusion. With that we resign ourselves to living a half-dead life, assuming this is just the way things have to be.

It takes courage to hang onto this longing—no matter how late in the game it may seem—and believe that more can be had. But for that to happen, we must be willing to become alive. And to do that, we'll need to face our Fear of Self.

The Big Vicious Circle

Why are we afraid to let go? Why do we fear that if we don't stay hyper-vigilant, constantly watching for what could go wrong, something bad might happen? What is the dangerous something we fear will surface from the depths of our spontaneous being?

When it comes down to it, there are basically two things that could happen. One, there's the possibility that some terrible monster will come out of us. Something destructive will rear its ugly head. Two, there's the possibility that something wonderfully creative and pleasurable will surface. Something constructive and life-expanding will bubble up.

While it's easy to imagine why we might fear the first possibility, it's not true that this is the only option that frightens us. Sure, fear of our negativity is one good reason to baton down the hatches on our free-wheeling soul movements. For chances are good, we're sitting on a powder keg of hate and hostility, anger and resentment, and cruel impulses buried inside. These we quite understandably fear letting out.

And make no mistake, they exist in every human being to one degree or another. They exist to the degree our positive expressions have been interrupted when we are young. Full expression of our life force is first prohibited by our parents and others around us, under the misguided belief that allowing us to express ourselves might lead to danger. Later, we do the repressing of our own selves.

So let's be clear: Once we become adults, we are no longer constrained by our past. Rather, we continue to hold ourselves back by reigning in our natural constructive life force that was, once upon a time, forbidden by someone else.

Here we go then, launched into one of the most famous vicious circles there is, caused by an error imposed upon us by the mere fact of what it means to be born a human. For when positive forces are held back, negative forces grow instead. What's really happening here is that a positive force becomes twisted and distorted, disturbing its original essence and converting it into a negative force. This now-negative force isn't a different force that has just come into existence. Our rage, for example, is not a new energy current or emotion. No, our rage is made from the same original substance as our love. And if we'll let it, it can turn back into love.

In truth, this can happen fairly easily, since any negative emotion will readily convert back to its original natural form. To do this with our rage requires we first admit it exists, and then we need to fully experience it, doing so under proper circumstances so this is done in a way that doesn't hurt someone else. As we allow ourselves to fully identify with powerful feelings such as rage, we want to keep a sense of proportion about it. It's important we don't turn toward rejecting our total personality because it exists. Then, and only then, our rage can be restored to the warmth of pleasurable and loving feelings.

Along the way, we may need to traverse other temporary emotions, including sadness, self-pity and pain. We'll also probably need to reconnect with our healthy aggression and self-assertion. Basically, we're going to need to own up to all our negative energy currents and experience them. And we'll need to allow them to exist for as long as they naturally exist. That's the way to transform what's unnatural and destructive back its original loving face.

The Way Out

Let's go back to that vicious circle for a moment. For that's what we're living with when we avoid the healthy procedure just outlined. Bottomline: The bigger our rage, the greater our fear of it will be. Hence, the more we stay on guard. And the more guarded we are, the less we are able to be spontaneous. And spontaneity is part of the formula for allowing our destructive emotions to return to their original state as pleasure currents. Sigh.

We have come to fear the destructive forces, which is understandable, but we often also fear the forces of pleasure and love, maybe even more so. We fear them because they ask us to remain unguarded, and to trust our inner spontaneous nature. Remember, that's the only way for the love forces to be kept alive, by our being totally unafraid of ourselves. To give up being guarded, though, seems like asking for annihilation, because then we're letting something other than our watchful ego work in cooperation with the process of living.

What's it going to take to unwind this vicious circle? It all hinges on meeting what we fear. And what we fear are the love forces that require we give up our tight grip on life, where our watchful eyes are hoping to control and manipulate life, wringing all the spontaneity out of it. The further along we go, holding on for dear life, the more emptiness and frustration build, causing anger and rage to grow. In the end, fear of self grows too.

We will remain caught in this vicious cycle as long as we refuse to take the steps needed to overcome our resistance to meeting our fear. And typically, at the top of our list of things we want to avoid is dealing with our fears. Yet, if we can make a start in facing the self—and sorry to say, this will mean doing more than making some kind of general nod toward the existence of our negative feelings—the relief and liberation will make our efforts worth it.

Once we get underway, we'll see that doing this work of self-discovery is neither as dangerous nor as difficult as we might imagine it to be. Our steps in this direction are blessed, and they will allow our life to open up. Our pent-up emotions must be lived through to be transformed, but bear in mind, this doesn't mean we go around acting out our anger. That will only lead to retaliation. We must seek out therapeutic supervision where our inner expressions will not cause outer harm.

The more we take responsibility for our destructive feelings, acknowledging them and expressing them safely, the less will we feel compelled to act them out. We will stop over-reacting to situations as happens so often in our daily lives, and we will no longer inadvertently and indirectly spread our anger onto others. We all do this way more than we realize.

The more quickly we get through this work of self-transformation, the sooner our experience of greater pleasure can take place. But for as long as fear of self exists, it will be impossible to feel fulfilled. Absolutely impossible.

Giving and Receiving

We all need the sustenance of affection, warmth and acceptance of our uniqueness in order to thrive. But when our need to receive these things goes unfulfilled, our psyche takes a hit. For just as our bodies need pleasure, so do our souls. Without it, our growth will be stunted.

As children, we were all dependent on having our needs met by others. We needed to receive. In addition, children have a need to give. So while we readily recognize the frustration that came from not receiving enough, we tend to overlook the frustration of not sufficiently giving. As we grow up, it is understood that a child who didn't receive enough may find it difficult to give of themselves, but usually we stop there. To better heal the damage of not receiving enough—beyond realizing that we are not helpless regarding our past and we can now establish a new balance—we must also recognize that a far worse pain of frustration was created when we couldn't give what we had.

By overly focusing on the aspect of lack of receiving, a generation of self-pitying people has been created who felt they'd been shortchanged by life because they didn't receive enough. They became parents who were emotionally crippled, and this led to over-giving in the next generation. Rather than feeling the pain of their frustration and seeking to find a healthy balance, they created a generation of helicopter parents.

The continuum of giving and receiving is a soul movement that must flow. And in order for us to be healthy and to feel fulfilled, we need to be part of this ongoing process. We do that by allowing these forces to function, passing positive forces onto others and receiving what others are letting flow into us.

So the possibility always exists for us to give in a healthy way. Instead, too often we heap more pain onto our heads by withholding what we have to give. This pain is actually far worse than the pain of not having received enough.

Think of it this way. If more of anything builds up, a tension will be created. And this overfullness is not going to feel good. So if we are holding back our Real Self because we feel fear, we're going to feel that tension. As such, we are pained as much by our not giving as by whatever it is we complain about not getting.

For a long time, religion has taken the lopsided approach of over-emphasizing giving: *It's more blessed to give than to receive.* By constantly stressing the need to give love, give mercy or give understanding, loving seems to be a pious command that is fulfilled by way of sacrifice. People go on to develop the hidden belief that to love is to impoverish oneself. If we don't suffer in our loving or shortchange ourselves in some fashion, it's not considered real love.

To this day, many people's unconscious concept of love includes certain actions that go against their own best interests. In short, love is seen as a pleasureless, sacrificial, depriving act that impoverishes us for the sake of being "good." No wonder we fear loving. Religions have historically also denied the pleasurable feelings that love causes in the body, accusing them of being sinful. From this perspective, people must either give into its spontaneous manifestations and become "wicked," or we cut out the very feelings that make up its force and love as an unpleasant duty. No wonder love is rejected.

Many people have spurned such a false concept of love, only to swing over to the other extreme, remaining greedy, selfish children who insist on receiving exclusively and without needing to give in the least. These are the two undesirable extremes that humanity bounces between. If we search with self-honesty for both sides within, we're apt to find both of these distortions.

In either case, there must be a fear of self. Otherwise the natural urge to give abundantly would arise. We would give as abundantly and generously as all of nature does! This would happen on the material level all the way down to the most subtle levels.

This equation always comes out correct: The greater our natural inclination to give, the less will be our tendencies for self-deprivation, masochistic withholding and suffering; the more we embrace false giving through self-impoverishment and lack of self-assertion, the less will there be a spontaneous flow of real generosity.

We can ask ourselves: Where am I holding onto an old grudge or an old perspective that leaves others out due to a resentment or some kind of censorship? Am I willing to allow a new attitude to surface from the depths of myself, to see things in a new light? When the latter happens, it does so naturally and not by force. It makes room for seeing a new reality about someone else that makes the old grudge meaningless. It sees no shame in giving up a useless scrap of pride. It finds no lack of character in having compassion and forgiving.

This is the way forward—by way of many seemingly small incidents—to loosen the grip of our withholding that's responsible for far more pain than any lack of receiving. Once we get this ball rolling, it will become easier and easier to allow the natural flow of warm feelings. But at one point, we're going to have to make a choice: Do I want to stick with my old ways, excluding and resenting and restricting, or do I want to welcome and follow a new strength from within?

Watch for such decision points. For needless to say, we're going to need to notice when the point of decision appears. But rest assured, they will be right there on the surface, easy to spot. These are never lost in our unconscious the way some other material can get lost. It's just that most of the time, we prefer to gloss over them.

When we find ourselves standing at the point of such a decision, it may feel like we're out on a ledge. The new way may look scary and risky. The old way—the cold way of separation—may seem safe. But really, can that even be true? Giving ourselves over to an apparently new force will be like stepping off into the great unknown. We might be able to sense the liberation of it, but still it will cause us to fear…what's next?

If we can let go enough to give up our destructive attitude, whatever that might be, we will embark on a whole new way of living: We'll start living from the inside out. This is the healing we've been seeking and hoping for. This is the how it comes about. It can't come any other way.

A New Way

Let's not kid ourselves, the first steps won't be easy. We'll waffle there, teetering on the cusp. This is a good time to notice how we exclude ourselves, how by tightly holding on, we constrict the flow. When we see ourselves there at that cusp, we can become aware of where our options will take us. We can go the old constricting way, with all its rigidity and pat formulas for how things should be. Or we can sit back and watch new vistas open up. We don't need to pressure ourselves. Just observe.

By remembering what each way means, we'll become ready to let go of the old way that refuses life, that limits love, and that foregoes happiness and unfoldment and giving forth of our riches. We will start to form a new understanding that makes room for others.

If we don't stop the flow, the new way will steadily increase. This beautiful flowing movement contains a self-regulating mechanism that we can totally trust. To whatever degree we are willing to let go of our self-centered, self-destructive and self-pitying attitudes, to that degree our fear of self will automatically diminish. Something new will start to take over from within. The creative powers will spring to life. We won't keep putting the brakes on our own life force.

As a result, we won't keep inflicting painful frustration upon ourselves. We'll be filled with the immense pleasure of following our natural inner movement. We'll be able to experience the joy of both giving and receiving.

When a vessel is closed, it can't be filled any more than it can be emptied. As long as we remain in the old closed position of refusing and isolating, we can't receive. As long as we won't let go of our self-imposed limitations, we make it impossible to give. By holding ourselves guarded and tight, we don't actually protect ourselves from danger, and what's more, we seal ourselves off from the healthy universal forces—those that would love to stream into us, and those that would gladly come streaming out of us.

May these words help us on our journey to experiencing fulfillment. May they kindle a spark that lights our way when we face the decision point between holding on tightly and gently letting go. Little by little, may we relinquish everything that bars our way to our final destination.

"Be blessed, be in peace, be in God."
–The Pathwork Guide

Chapter 2

Fully Facing our Fear of Loving

As we've probably heard by now, love is the greatest power there is. Every spiritual teaching or philosophy, along with every religious scholar and psychology professor, proclaims this truth: Love is the one and only power. If you've got it, you are mighty, strong and safe. Without it, you are separate, scared and poor.

Sounds simple enough. Yet this knowledge doesn't really help us unless we've discovered where—deep down inside—we can't love or won't love. Why is it that we resist loving? Unless we sort out the answer to this question, no eternal truth about love can possibly help us.

If we've already made some progress on our search for inner knowing, we've probably already run headlong—after considerable digging and exploring—into our fear of loving. Becoming aware of such a fear is quintessential for taking further steps. It's not enough to have a theoretical understanding that such a fear of loving exists; we have to actually experience this fear. For people who don't yet wish to know themselves, such an awareness will not yet exist.

But even for those of us who have become aware of this inner conflict, we may not yet fully comprehend the why of it. *Why am I so afraid of loving?* Let's explore some of the facets of this perplexing phenomenon, a topic we'll return to in future teachings when we illuminate this very basic problem from other angles.

Let's start with this: Those who cannot love are immature. And when we are immature, we are not living in reality. To live a life based on unreality, then, must lead to conflict and unhappiness, for where there is untruth there is ignorance and darkness.

Maturity, as such, means essentially having the ability to love.

Alas, we all hold fragmented aspects within ourselves that are trapped in childhood states. And these child parts require an unlimited amount of love. For these child fragments are one-sided, unreasonable, demanding, and lacking in understanding, as all immature creatures are. Its laundry list of impossible wants includes: to be loved by everyone, to be loved 100%, to be instantly satisfied, and to be loved in spite of our selfish, unreasonable ways. This, in a nutshell, is why we are afraid of loving.

Since this child inside us demands complete surrender from others, thinking surely this would mean being loved, how can the child help but resist surrendering? Our inner child makes us want to reign supreme over the very ones who are supposed to love us, which would effectively turn them into our submissive little slaves.

Sometimes, it turns out, we become the ones who are submissive emotional slaves. This happens when we feel we absolutely must have love, acceptance or agreement from a specific person, but we're also aware we might not get it. Fearing rejection and defeat, it may seem that such submissive behavior is our only chance. And since, on a superficial level some of our submissive behavior may resemble true love, it's easy for us to deceive ourselves—especially when we're mired in such a dismal, desperate state—into believing that when we submit, we truly love.

In other words, we often unconsciously craft our own inner idea of what love is, which vaguely resembles what's taught in some religions and philosophies. To us, it seems that when we submit we are not being selfish and we are offering some kind of sacrifice. It seems the other person is now the center of our world. While there is some truth to this, it's not true in essence. In truth, we remain our center.

Our desire is to convince the other to love us, according to our childish concept of what love is. They are supposed to worship us, follow our every whim, give up their own self-direction and allow the child in us to rule. And yes, this is the same child in us who cries inwardly any time its wishes are not met. Is it any wonder we're afraid to love, when all these unconscious demands are hiding out in our psyche?

And since our concepts equating love with slavish submission are unconscious, they are so much more powerful than our conscious beliefs. Ergo, we do not wish to love. For we don't wish to follow another's will. We don't wish to give up our own autonomy, submitting to someone else's rule.

It's only when we can recognize our own childish distorted ideas about love that we can start to see the childish demands of another for what they are. And only then will we stop being influenced by them, no longer feeling obligated to give in, or guilty if we do not. That's when we'll start to see that perhaps another kind of love can be given, one that is more detached and less needy and demanding.

Also, once we discover the unfair demands of the child inside us, we can begin to reason with it. We will realize that we have a misunderstanding about love that is seriously different from real love. Once we see this, we won't be so afraid to love. We'll realize that loving doesn't mean we give up our dignity or self-government; loving does not mean lack of freedom.

If we stop making childish demand, little by little we'll learn to love maturely. And then we can expect the same in return. There is no danger in loving this way. We remain free and do not become enslaved. It's really as simple and logical as that. When we give up our childish ideas of how we think others should love us, we will no longer fear loving them.

A Gradual Process

Learning to love is a gradual process of growing and maturing. We will not instantly enjoy the majestic, all-encompassing love our soul is striving for. For the child in us only knows extremes. This creates a giant conflict in our soul of yearning for great love and simultaneously hiding from it. We're either in the heights of love—*We've reached the final goal!*—or we have nothing.

The more we try to thwart the healthy instincts of the striving side, the stronger it's going to clamor to be heard. This creates a vague inner feeling of discontent, like we're missing something but can't quite put our finger on it. One part of our psyche will end up sabotaging the rightful demands of the other part. And since we fall short of reaching our desire, we withdraw altogether. This is caused by the either/or tendencies of the immature parts of ourselves, as well as by our flare for the dramatic. *If I can't have what I want, then I don't want anything!* Here come the crocodile tears.

As we become more mature, we'll come to realize that we can only attain true fulfillment of love by starting out on the lower rungs of the ladder. Maybe we should start by letting other people feel about us as they wish. If we can offer this kind of authentic "permission," we will be on our way to giving up our demands without feeling hostile. We'll discover it's possible to truly like and respect others, even if they don't bend to our will. This may not sound like much. We might even think this doesn't apply to us. But are we sure? Really and truly?

When things go wrong, that's the time to test our emotions. As we evaluate our feelings, we might discover the child in us is working overtime. But now we have new tools for addressing what's happening. When we can give up our subtle forcing current, we will feel an entirely new kind of emotional reaction inside. We will feel as though a tremendous burden has been lifted from us.

The next step will be to let go of any remaining hostility, once we've become aware of it through our process of inner healing work. When this occurs, we'll find a new respect and liking for anyone who did not grant us their "unconditional surrender," which is what we unconsciously wanted and were not happy about when we didn't get it. It will feel like a tight band dissolving within. Now we can set others free, liking and respecting them as people, but without needing to possess their love or their admiration.

Friends, this probably won't look like much from the outside. But this is a decisive step that in reality is more dramatic than something we can see. It will launch us on our way up the relationship ladder toward heights that can one day be ours. But we must not skip this initial undramatic and seemingly trivial step. Without this step, we can never reach our final goal. At the same time, we're not yet ready to stand on the top rung.

When we're just starting to make our way up the ladder, we're not yet able to forget ourselves completely. We've still got some vanity and a certain amount of selfishness we need to contend with. Let's not get discouraged because we can't pole vault all the way to the top. Our goal is to learn about our emotions through the painstaking steps of careful analysis, letting them mature gradually, organically.

It doesn't work to skip steps. If we are patient with ourselves, our goals of loving are attainable. But first, before we can love others, we need to learn to like and respect them, even when we don't get what we want. And to do that, we must first figure out where, deep inside, we really haven't done that at all.

Developing Intuition

How do we tell the difference between real, ideal love and sham love— the wrong, weak submissiveness—that poses as love? They can look so deceptively similar! For it's that sham love that scares us, not the real thing.

For starters, we have to find for ourselves where and how we stray from the straight and narrow, through our unspoken demands and unrealistic expectations. It will not be enough to sense real love just by reading about it. This is true for everyone, no exceptions.

As long as the child in us keeps subtly pushing to get its way, trying to emotionally and unconsciously force others to submit, we are lost in wishful thinking. We will build unreal castles in our minds that may not even be in a place we want to live. We construct these unreal situations that are hazardous to inhabit, and then we turn a blind eye to how we are doing this. We don't see what we are doing because we don't want to. And then we wonder why we can't rely on our own judgment or intuition.

Our psyches are not fools. Our psyche knows perfectly well that our radar is off, that we're not reading people as they really are in relation to us, or the situation as a whole the way it really is. But we don't want to see the truth. So, not surprisingly, we aren't able to trust our judgment. Beyond that, we don't trust that the other person is going to live up to our expectations. Our unrealistic expectations, that is.

This is what we use to justify not loving. For how can we love someone we can't trust? In truth, in order to trust someone, we have to be able to see if that person or situation calls for it. Maybe we'd be better served to simply offer respect and affection, and leave it at that.

It's only by giving up a little bit of what we want—unconsciously, most of the time—that we will be able to see what is. That's the way to see reality. With this new set of lenses, we can now begin to discern intelligently and follow our intuition. We will start to have respect for ourselves and our ability to give up something we want, without becoming hostile about it. With our new clarity, we will be able to deal with situations in our lives like adults.

This is how we learn to trust: trust ourselves, trust our judgment and trust other people. Without the windstorm of our forcing current, we won't overestimate others, but instead observe them and feel what is true. This is a far cry better than our usual habit of believing only what we want to be true.

Once we've practiced this kind of "trust fall" for a while, loving won't feel like such a danger. Until then, we'll remain deliberately blind. For our immature parts will continue to think that by willing something, we make it so. As such, our choices will continue to be untrustworthy. That's what makes us shy away from loving even more, all the while sticking our heads in the clouds pretending there is no danger to us in being loved.

Our goal is to become objective in the way we evaluate others, and to learn to let go with grace. All we're letting go of is our self-willed forcing currents that can never serve our highest good. This will allow us to learn how to respect someone, even if they thwart our will. We'll stop building castles in the sky that obstruct our view of what's really happening.

For when we do that, we're not only ignoring reality, we're rejecting it. But if we want to be able to rely on our intuition, we're going to need to see what is real, right in front of our face. When we can do this—see with mature eyes—we will be able to trust ourselves.

This is what it looks like to accept reality, accepting that Earth life isn't perfect. This is how we learn to cope with life and make the best of it. Our work is to take the general concept that "life isn't perfect" and put it to practical use in some aspect of ourselves. Sometimes people aren't going to like us, and we have to accept this apparent imperfection in our reality. This is a safer way to walk in the world that will unwind the vicious circles we've been creating with our demand that everyone must feel about us as we wish.

Intuition is not for chumps. It's the highest sense perception that we humans can reach. But we'll never reach it as long as the hidden child in us goes undetected and running wild. To be clear, as long as we remain human, our intuition will never be 100% perfect. Yet simply by being aware of this reality—by being willing to say, "I'm not entirely sure, I could be wrong here"— we become willing to learn from our mistakes. And suddenly our ignorance becomes harmless.

Having the concise, conscious thought, "I don't know," is powerful. Within it lies the potential to eventually learn, see and know. But our intuition will never become a wall we can blindly lean on with 100% certainty and total confidence. And that's why it's so valuable. That's why we must work to open it up as best we can, while staying humble enough to realize we can't know everything.

When we consult our own intuition, without any forcing current or wishful thinking to muddy the water, we will sense certain potentials, and we'll also sense certain limitations. Beyond that, life is a question mark. With such a framing approach, we promote an attitude of openness and readiness to watch life and the people in it. Developing this kind of perception will bear a lot of fruit for us. Plus, it's a sign of maturity. Because only the immature must have immediate answers. It's the inner child who needs to nail down everything, not leaving any room for unanswered questions or doubt.

Through our willingness to hang out in open spaces—to live with unanswered questions—we'll develop the courage needed to be in reality, to accept what is. This will lead to more self-respect, better intuition, greater discernment and improved awareness. Then we'll be able to trust and we'll do so wisely. Best of all, when the right situation is at hand, we'll have no fear of loving. See how this is all tied together with one string?

Prayer and Patience

We have these lofty ideas of what it looks like to love. We like to imagine only the highest, most perfect kind. But this ignores the reality that there are many stages of love that lead up to this. Love comes in many varieties. But in the ignorance of our immaturity, we'll avoid the kind of love we're actually capable of giving right now, and then miss it altogether when something similar is offered to us.

So how should we proceed? After all, we may know perfectly well that our emotions aren't working quite right, and we might truly desire to change, but then what? How do we go about re-educating these young inner parts and growing ourselves up?

First, our desire for change shouldn't come with a truckload of pressure. It doesn't work to rush. Rather, we need to adopt a calmness about all this, because emotions, quite frankly, are not quick to change.

What we need to discover is where, how and why our emotions are not in truth. We also need to become aware of where we're confused. What exactly are our unanswered inner questions? And last but not least, we have to let go of our resistance to seeing ourselves as we really and truly are, right now. We have to become willing to be honest with ourselves.

Prayer, if we understand how to properly use it, works in a similar way. When we pray, we can ask for help to face ourselves, and to understand our current problems. Our prayers should not be for huge, unattainable goals, but rather that we can see what's happening in our seemingly small daily disharmonies. This is the path forward for gaining deeper insight into ourselves.

And where should we be directing these prayers? Not up into the sky. No, we want to aim our prayers toward our own unconscious. For this is where God lives: deep down inside of us. By directing our prayers at the divine spark within, we are also reaching the parts of ourselves that are most hidden from our conscious awareness.

Our goal is to strengthen the parts of our psyche that are healthy, while at the same time weakening the unhealthy childish parts that are resistant. So our prayers should deal with what we wish to uncover, asking to see where we have strayed from the truth due to our lack of understanding. As we sit with a calm and quiet mind, we can let go of any urgency or tension. Keep in mind, change and growth can only come when we go slow and steady.

Patience we are taught, after all, is a virtue. Of course, as people often do, we may try to make a virtue out of a fault. So sometimes we deceive ourselves into thinking we're being patient when in fact we're just not making an effort. Or we might be impatient and we tell ourselves we're just being active or energetic. The challenge is to figure out what's really going on.

So why does impatience hinder us and the fulfillment of our ambitions? Because it's yet another form of immaturity. It's that little child inside us who wants everything, our way, right now. It's the child who cannot wait. The problem is that the child lives in the now, but does so in the wrong way. It has no sense of a tomorrow, so it thinks that whatever doesn't happen immediately will never happen.

If we're mature, however, we can wait. A mature person can understand that if our desired goal doesn't get accomplished right now, there must be some reason for the delay. Some of those reasons might reside in the self, and if that's the case we can use the waiting time constructively, searching for them and eliminating them. Whatever time we have to spend waiting can be used to gain the insight, ability or understanding we've been lacking. In this way, patience truly can work to our advantage.

True patience comes with genuine discernment. Perhaps in one instance it's best to just wait. At another time, it could be better to take action. However it goes, know this: When we are deep in our inner work, we're going to need to have patience. For concentrated inner healing does not instantly relate to outer manifestation. At times, we may need to act even as we are inwardly being patient. At other times we may need to be outwardly inactive while maintaining an inner state of patience.

How exactly are we defining patience here? To be patient means to know that we can't always have exactly what we want when we want it. It doesn't feel hindered by the tension and anxiety in our soul. For when we are feeling impatient, we also feel an inner pressure and tension and anxiety, all of which are based on feeling inadequate. There's a sense that "I won't be able to do this," whatever "this" might be. That's what it feels like to be impatient.

Patience then can only exist in a mature person who feels secure and who knows their limitations. At the same time, we must know our potential and trust ourselves. So when we aim for greater maturity, we'll receive many additional assets, including patience.

The Unconscious

If we ignore these teachings about the power of what lies hidden in our unconscious, we will continue to be baffled by the problems in our lives. But if we attempt to work with these teachings at only a superficial level, we're apt to become frustrated, as life keeps producing one painful episode after another. As a result, our sense of inadequacy will grow instead of go away.

So where exactly is the dividing line between the conscious and the unconscious mind? And what regulates what stays down and what comes up? In fact, there's no strict line between the two parts. What we'll notice when we begin to do our work of self-discovery however is that we expected to uncover things that were completely unknown to us. But then, when we do find a new recognition, it has a familiar feel to it. We'll see something in a new light and we will have a new understanding about its significance, but it won't feel entirely new. It's just that until now, we kept looking away from it. But it was always there.

It was caught somewhere in a no-man's land between our conscious thoughts and our unconscious notions, where there's a fading transition, if you will. Perhaps we can imagine our whole psyche or mind as a big round ball. The more self-development work we have done on ourselves—i.e., the more evolved we have become—the clearer this sphere will be, with no haze or fog.

For a less developed person, a large portion of their ball will be fogged in. In that case, the part that functions on a conscious level will be the smaller area inside the ball. When we raise our level of consciousness, what we're really doing is lifting more of ourselves out of the fog. Over time, the haze will recede, and we'll have more clarity as we become more and more conscious.

The universe we need to explore is inside us. And since we are a truly a universe onto ourselves, the only way for us to reach universal consciousness is through this process of self-finding, which is what lifts us out of the fog. We won't be able to gain such consciousness by learning things with our brains alone.

Make no mistake, our brains are valuable tools for doing the work of self-finding, and that's what we must do if we want the fog to clear. But our deeper work of self-discovery is the doorway we must pass through to find unity. Our self-knowing will be the common denominator that will unite everything: all sciences and every religion. Until then, all our human knowledge and achievements will keep operating in separate silos.

Over time, as humanity has developed and awakening has continued, we are learning more and more to perceive our inner universe, with all its infinite possibilities. This is what has allowed us to open up our understanding of the larger universe and all its laws, spiritual as well as material. Just as outside, inside us is a logical world that operates according to just laws. Only when we sense this truth can we also truly sense God and God's creation.

Fear, Truth & Flexibility

So much of what holds us back is our fear of the unknown. But the unknown will become known to us if we are willing to navigate the treacherous terrain of our own inner landscape. This means, we're going to have to take this task of self-searching very seriously. It's not enough to read these words. They can do no more than provide us with the incentive to begin. We must actually experience the presence of our immature emotions in action. When we do this, the unknown will become known to us. Even the parts that continue to be unknown to us won't be able to frighten us any more, once we admit, "I don't know." That small shift will make an enormous difference.

As we become familiar with this process, we will stop seeing self-responsibility and self-government as a "must" that our inner child rejects. We'll no longer run away from the apparent danger of facing the unknown. Instead it will be a privilege and a freedom to see ourselves in truth.

It's our fear of the unknown that makes us distort true concepts into their fixed opposite. But truth, by its very nature, is flexible. It cannot be fixed. Nothing that is true can be rigid or static. It's always fluid. And this flexibility appears to us as a threat. We want the pseudo-safety of a stone wall we can lean on. This tendency, in fact, is what caused religions to distort beautiful teachings into dogma.

Rigidity has a way of satisfying our irrational, unfounded fears. We think that if something is fixed, that makes it safe, and that what's flexible is unsafe. But truth, like anything else that is alive, is a living thing that must be flexible. As a result, people fear truth. We fear light. We fear life. The idea that flexibility is unsafe is one of the greatest illusions of this world.

When we reach the point where we no longer fear self-responsibility because we've lost our self-contempt and our mistrust in ourselves, then we will no longer fear living in a flexible universe. We won't need rigid rules that we can cling to. Flexible laws won't feel like a danger to us. It's the child in us who doesn't dare assume self-responsibility that wants inflexible laws to follow.

Our fear of the unknown rises up from our insecurities: *Will I be able to cope? Is my judgment adequate? Will I have the right reactions? Am I going to make a mistake? Dare I make a mistake?* In other words, our deepest fear of the unknown is really about not knowing ourselves. As we get to know all of ourselves, we will lose this fear, along with fear of self-responsibility. And then we'll no longer fear the truth of the flexible spiritual laws that guide the universe. Better yet, we'll no longer fear life, which is incredibly flexible, like, all the time.

In the last analysis, by its very nature, flexibility is unchangeable. That's life.

Are All Fears Bad?

By now, we've used the word "fear" a bunch of times, and we've talked about "irrational fears." Does this mean there is such a thing as a "rational fear?" Yes, there is. For if we are in some kind of danger, our reaction to fear will be healthy. It acts like a signal, giving us a heads up that we need to do something to save ourselves from danger. In this situation, our fear is constructive, not destructive. Without such an inner red alert, we would be destroyed. But that is decidedly different from the unhealthy destructive fears that populate our psyche and which we've been talking about here.

This is connected with our instincts. How is it we come to mismanage our natural instincts when it comes to fear? It comes down to a question of trust in the self. If there are distorted ideas and emotions in our unconscious that cause us to thwart our instincts, we won't trust them. What can happen is that we realize our fears have been unjustified. And so we stop heeding them altogether, even though there may have been a good reason to listen to them.

Consequently, we will find ourselves even more consumed by fear, now not knowing when we can trust our instincts or intuition, and when we should not. But after we resolve our unfounded reasons for being fear-ridden, when fear does come up we will have the maturity to question it thoughtfully, instead of doing what we've always done: bury it.

We may also have heard the word "fear" used in connection with God. For example, we read in Scripture that "the fear of the Lord is the beginning of wisdom." This "fear of God" also has absolutely nothing in common with healthy protective fear. All references in the Bible to fear of God are due to translation errors. But it's not entirely an accident that such mistakes were made.

The deeper reason for this error has to do with a combination of the God-image and our fear of the unknown. On one hand, we think we need a strong authority who will uphold fixed rules because then we won't have to take on any self-responsibility. But on the other hand, this creates an unhealthy fear, which is what unavoidably happens when we don't attain maturity and self-responsibility. Whether we fear life, ourselves, other people or an avenging God, it all amounts to the same thing.

In addition to this, there is a simple misunderstanding going on here regarding certain times in the Bible. In short, back then the word "fear" meant something different. Today, we might best describe its meaning as "honor" or "respect." And the respect to be paid to the highest intelligence, love and wisdom there is goes beyond words. Were we to be in the presence of such unlimited greatness, any being would stand in awe, but not in fear. For such a wonder surpasses all understanding. That sentiment is what the word "fear" was attempting to convey, but fell far short.

"Be blessed, all of you, my dear ones. May you find the way to maturity and love by finding where, how, and why you do not love now. May you find the courage to free yourself of this unnecessary burden of fearing love and life. Go in peace, my dearest friends, be in God."

–The Pathwork Guide

Chapter 3

Finding Freedom and Peace by Overcoming Fear of the Unknown

Life is a trap, of a kind, stuck as we are in this struggle to overcome the duality between life and death. From this fundamental predicament stem all our other problems, fears and tensions. It shows up in our fear of death, of course, as well as in our fear of aging and our fear of the unknown. What's the common root of all these fears? The passage of time.

In an effort to deal with these basic fears, humanity has devised various philosophies and spiritual or religious concepts. But even if these concepts are true, evolving perhaps from someone's attempts to pass on a true experience, they're not going to do the trick in relieving our tension. Truth be told, the only way to truly overcome our fears—to reconcile the great divide of this giant duality—is to dive deep into the mega-unknown we all fear so much: our own psyche.

Well, how hard could that be? Turns out, it sounds simpler than it is. For to explore the hidden corners of our own minds, we have to do more than resolve dualities. We're going to need to discover all the facets of our innermost selves, without glibly explaining away any tensions and disturbances we encounter along the way.

Our incentive is this: To the degree we are in the dark about what is going on inside, to that degree we will fear the passing of time; we will fear the great unknown. When we're young, it's easy to brush these things aside. But sooner or later, if we won't face ourselves, we'll come face-to-face with our fear of death. To the extent, however, that we know ourselves, we will feel fulfilled in life. And to that same degree death will not be feared. Instead, it will occur as an organic development, and the unknown will no longer seem like a threat.

Doing this work of self-discovery is no picnic, friends. Plus, there are escape hatches everywhere. If we look for them, we'll even find them within the framework of this particular path of growth and healing. The only way then to succeed in unifying ourselves is by ruthlessly searching to see, evaluate and understand ourselves.

There are lots of obstacles to contend with on the road to freedom from fear of death. One of the main hurdles is our fear of letting go of the separating barriers between us and the opposite sex. As long as these hurdles remain in place, our fear of death will exist just as strongly. There is, in fact, a direct connection between three specific fears:

1) Fear of our self and what's hiding in our own unconscious.

2) Fear of loving a person of the opposite sex.

3) Fear of death.

Perhaps the connection between the first two is beginning to dawn on us, but this third addition to the triad may seem like a novel idea. Let's explore this some more so we can know the truth being revealed by these words.

Being All We Can Be

To experience self-fulfillment, we're going to need to fulfill ourselves as either a man or a woman. Ultimately, to do that, we'll need to overcome whatever barriers there are between us and the opposite sex. To be sure, this isn't the only aspect necessary for self-fulfillment. Perhaps we need to become aware of certain talents we possess, or some good quality like courage or resourcefulness. Maybe we need to discover how broadminded we are, or creative.

But none of these can really, truly blossom unless a man becomes a man, and a woman becomes a woman. For whatever self-realization we may accomplish while barriers to union with another are still in place will not be

100% complete. Because what such barriers are pointing to are the barriers within, which are blocking off an area of the self we are avoiding exploring and understanding.

Think of it as a sign we aren't fully ready to grow up and instead insist that some part of us remain stuck in infancy. When all our resistance to seeing these previously unknown parts of ourselves is gone, then we will no longer fear ourselves. And once our fear of self has vanished, we can't possibly fear anyone else, whether they are the same sex as us or a member of the opposite sex.

Freeing ourselves from unrealistic attitudes will also release our fierce grip of control that prevents us from letting go into a state of being. That same tight grip stands in the way of entering the cosmic stream of timelessness, which is what we experience when we are in the highest states of bliss with a partner. This is also what we experience in the great bliss that we call death.

Death has a lot of faces. For those of us who are afraid, tightly holding onto our little self, we might experience seclusion and separateness as a form of death. By contrast, if we are fully alive and living free of fear, no longer bent on preserving the little self, we can experience death with the same kind of glory as union on this Earth!

So we must tackle this struggle for self-realization from three sides. First, we need to remove the barriers that exist between the conscious and unconscious areas of our psyche. Second, we must remove the barriers that arise between ourselves and our partners, whoever they are at this phase of our journey. Third, we need to look at the barriers that exist between us and the cosmic stream.

When we are being carried by this stream, it will seem that all is right with the world. It's when we fear ourselves, other people and the stream of life that's carrying us all forward, that we don't trust the passing of time. Instead, we hold on for dear life to our little egoic self, creating walls of fog between us and our higher consciousness.

The Big Triad: Pride, Self-Will and Fear

The clouds that hinder living fully in the current moment are made up of basically three things: pride, self-will and fear. In one way or another, all our faults and confusions, conflicts and misconceptions are derived from these three hindrances. And this same triad blocks the three routes to self-realization we just mentioned. Let's look at this more closely.

What's the big barrier between consciousness and the unconscious? Pride. It bars the door because, let's face it, we're not going to be thrilled by what we find in there. It won't be flattering, shall we say. Even if what we find isn't all that bad, we still fear it might be. After all, we sure were hoping that absolutely everybody was going to admire us, all the time. This is the reason we so often pick up the values of the people whose approval we want. But when we do this, we create a wall of pride, a cloud bank that hinders having insight.

Self-will makes us apprehensive about what we'll uncover because we don't want to be forced to do something that our little ego doesn't like. Further, we're not excited about giving up anything we're not yet willing to surrender. Our self-will wants our little ego to stay in control, thank you very much, so we can keep clinging to the known.

And lastly, fear pitches in to make us believe that reality is not to be trusted. *Better to stick with what I already know.* In truth, buried deep in our unconscious is a stream of cosmic reality, of cosmic events. If we enter into this stream, it can't help but bring us fulfillment, meaningfulness and happiness. But when we don't trust this stream and therefore hang on tightly to what we know, believing we might fare better than if we take a chance and let go into the unknown, then we build a wall of fear. And this fear is what blocks us from reaching full self-recognition.

This ubiquitous triad of pride, self-will and fear also comes up between ourselves and our partners, creating barriers there. Whether we are a man or a woman, pride pokes its head up because we fear the apparent helplessness—and the shame that comes with it—of giving over to a force that's greater than our little ego self. Anyone whose been in a relationship knows that loving is humbling business, making it, as such, the enemy of pride.

From the place of pride, we want to call all the shots. We want to direct all the action and control all the outcomes. We don't want to give ourselves over to any force, even if that force is incredibly desirable. So we all go through life desiring to love, while we're also busily trying to block it. Our hope is that we can find a compromise for these contradictory currents running through our soul.

No doubt, the force propelling us toward love is a big one. It comes from our deepest, innermost nature. But the antagonists of pride, self-will and fear conspire to push us away from love.

Self-will is also in opposition to love because it wants solo control. It doesn't want to give itself up. It won't let go. It seems to us—wrongly so, of course—that we are only safe when we have only ourselves to obey. To let go and love, then, seems to make no sense. But is this really so?

Being realistic and objective, and being able to relinquish control and fearlessly enter love, are highly compatible forces. In fact, they're interdependent. But we block the experience of love out of fear we'll lose our dignity—that our pride will be hurt—and we'll have to give up our selfhood. In other words, we fear we'll have to let go of our clamoring little ego self. In reality, we can only gain true dignity and selfhood when we're willing to give up our pride and our self-will.

The Triad on Death and Dying

Dying is really the ultimate relinquishing of self-direction. So in a strange sort of way, surrendering into death can seem somehow humiliating. As such, when we look at our attitude toward death, we're likely to once again be influenced by the triad of pride, self-will and fear.

As a means of avoiding the humbling truth that when it comes to death, the little self doesn't have total say, we hold tightly to our pride and our self-will, which effectively creates ever stronger waves of fear.

So here we are, faced with a seeming duality between giving up the self and gaining full possession of the self. It looks to be a paradox: Are we only trying to find ourselves so we can give ourselves up in union with another and then to death? The truth is this: We can't successfully give up something we haven't found; we can't freely let go of something we've never really possessed.

So then if death and dying are supposed to be so great—such a blissful experience—why do we think of them as being so dark? Why don't we have a death instinct that's as strong as the one pulling us to lose ourselves in love? How come we have to work so hard to overcome our fear of death? Why must we battle so hard against this great unknown?

There's a very good reason for things to be the way they are. For wouldn't it be easy to wish for death when life becomes hard, painful and unfulfilling? Truly, in the unfinished state we're in—ignorant and often in a blind state of terror—it sure would be tempting to escape into death. But death, unfortunately, wouldn't prove any different from life. Both are intrinsically the same.

And so, in order to avoid having us prematurely jump ship, our life instinct must be super strong. And that can only operate as long as death remains a big mystery, an unknown. Mere words can never take away our fear of the unknown, so our life instinct manages to continue to keep our feet on the planet. Rather than caving into destructive motives, we find the stamina to try and try again.

But eventually we will come to master life by coming to understand the self. In this way, we will make peace with the whole universe. And when we reach this point, it will finally also occur to us that death is not something we need to fear. For our fear only exists in direct proportion to our fear of living and loving. Now we can start to see how one could possibly transcend the duality of life and death. The illusion that they are opposites starts to fade.

Finding Peace

These words may only make sense once we no longer see life as a threat. Then we won't be needing to flee life and our life instinct can settle down.

Then our life instinct is no longer in opposition to a death instinct. As these merge, we will stop either rushing ahead or holding back.

For if we look closely, we'll see how we are perpetually fluctuating between attempting to hold back time, practically crouching in a fear-cramped position, and rushing headlong into the future because we just can't stand the present moment. Rare, indeed, is the day when we are in complete harmony with the cosmic stream of our lives and ourselves.

That's what it means to be at peace within ourselves, to be in harmony with God. We're not holding back, we're not pushing forward, but are dissolving into the stream of life. We are in full possession of ourselves but have no fear about giving up self-possession. This great combination is what we can experience when we are blessed to have found our mate. And we'll eventually, ultimately, have the privilege of experiencing such peace as we transition into another form of consciousness.

What's the key that turns the ignition and heads us in this direction? It all lies in the self-discovery that awaits us on many levels deep in our being. Too often what we do instead is project our inner ills onto others and the outside world, hoping to avoid what seems like a terrifying self-confrontation. While doing this appears to give us a certain temporary satisfaction, it leaves us with an empty bucket in the end.

If, instead, we'll keep chipping away at self-knowing, one little step at a time, we will one day dissolve the clouds and barriers that obstruct our view. The more we tap into the timeless stream of our higher consciousness, the more it will furnish us with the wisdom, rightness and truth that can help us navigate our way every day. Chances are, we'll tap into it and then lose it again. Perseverance will be required. But our contact with the life stream will inform us about the greater significance of all creation.

We can liken the truth to the sun, which all the other planets revolve around. There in the center, the truth burns brightly, even when it's covered over by clouds. The clouds, as we said, are made up of our pride, self-will and fear, plus our ignorance that has us pushing ahead of time or fighting against it. But in that precious moment when we perceive our truth, regardless how insignificant it may seem in the grand scheme of things, the clouds float away.

We'll be touched by the warmth that radiates from the truth of our higher consciousness. We'll have renewed strength and sense of well-being. We'll be filled with joyfulness and peace.

We can't wish away our fears, nor our pride and self-will, hoping this inner sun will shine regardless of what we do. It doesn't work that way. The truth is constantly ready to warm us and enliven us, but first, we've probably got some overcoming to do. Lip service will not take us very far. We don't have to be perfect. Actually, we are already perfect in a sense, whenever we're willing to come to terms with our current imperfections.

It's when we stop struggling against the self, thereby shedding the heavy burden of pride and pretense, that we become willing to change. It's then, when we also shed our self-will, that our variety pack of fears will start to evaporate like an ice cube sitting in the sun.

"Be in peace, be in yourself, and therefore in God!"
–The Pathwork Guide

Chapter 4

Finding True Abundance by Going Through Our Fear

If we boil it down, there are essentially two philosophies about this thing we call life, and they are apparent contradictions. One imparts the perspective that if we are truly mature, spiritually and emotionally, we need to learn to accept life on life's terms, and often those terms are hard to take. Our best approach will be to accept what we can't change. When we won't accept life, this theory says, we breed anxiety and disharmony, and our peace of mind will be destroyed by the tension this creates. We make our situation worse. So the gauge of a mature, well-rounded personality, from this perspective, is how well we are able to accept the inevitable. Are we OK with our destiny? And how cool are we with, say, death?

The other school of thought postulates we don't need to accept any of this unpleasantness. All this stuff about accepting hardship, including death, is totally unnecessary. Our only destiny is the one we create for ourselves. And whenever we decide, we can mold ourselves a new destiny. A better destiny. One in which we no longer suffer. Real spiritual awakening, this side says, comes with the awareness that we don't need to accept suffering, and unfathomable abundance can be had, right here, right now.

Talk about two sides of the street! How confusing is that? But if we search for both of these perspectives, we're likely to find them in just about any great spiritual teaching, including these from the Pathwork Guide.

At first glance, these two philosophies might appear mutually exclusive. But maybe they're not. Can we find a common denominator that brings them together and unites them? In fact, we can: it is fear.

It's like this. If our desire for happiness stems from our fear of unhappiness, we can never be happy. But if we want happiness just for the sake of being happy, then nothing will bar the door. It might seem small, but there's really an enormous difference between these two approaches.

Because here's how fear works: If we have fear, sooner or later we're likely to experience the very thing we fear in order to rid ourselves of the fear. If, however, we are able to discover the truth behind the fear—which is of course that there is nothing to fear in the first place—then we can shed our fear without having to experience it. But alas, we are typically slow to catch on to this insight, in which case we need to cozy up to the circumstances we fear until they lose their fearful roar.

In other words, as long as we desire something positive out of fear of its opposite—the negative—our fear will keep us from attaining what's positive. And folks, this reality is rampant here on this dualistic sphere we call home. Too often, we don't want the good stuff for the sake of the good stuff, we want it because we hope it will make the bad stuff go away. Let's break this down and look at some of our more popular desires.

We can start with the great whale of duality: life and death. These are really two sides of the same coin, or two facets of the same process. This means that by learning how to die—which is what it feels like when we accept something we don't like—we will find out there wasn't anything to fear. We'll discover that this thing we all fear so much, death, isn't real. There is simply no such thing as death. Furthermore, since these two are joined at the hip, if we fear death, we'll also fear life, and vice versa.

Let's make an additional connection regarding death. It's impossible to love—to truly love—if we fear death. Just take a look at how humans behave. Those who live their lives with great gusto and joy are the ones who aren't afraid of dying. But the more we shrink back due to our fear of death, the more we will be hanging onto life by our fingernails, not because we are enjoying life so much but because we are scared to death of, well, death. If this is us, we're not really living at all. We're barely hanging on.

Fear of dying, then, stops us from living. Yet it's only by deeply living that we learn that life is one long, unending process, and dying is just a temporary illusion. In truth, clinging to life is never going to bring us pleasure or a sense of meaningfulness. So these two things are also linked. The more we cling, the less we enjoy it. It's just a matter of degree.

And since nearly no one is completely clear of their fear of death—for when that's truly the case, we no longer have to incarnate here on this life-and-death merry-go-round—hardly anyone really and truly lives. That said, there are some who are largely free from this fear of death, and those are the ones making meaningful lives filled with pleasure.

Since all this is so hard for the average person to sort out on their own—to see that death is not something we need to fear—we have to keep showing up over and over, one life after another, and keep learning how to die until we can do it well. Until one day we get it: dying doesn't frighten us. Glory be, that's the day we arrive at life eternal, but not a day sooner. For as long as we fear death, we have to keep going through it.

Fear and Control

Another way we miss the mark in life is by always wishing to be in control. As a result, we perpetually fear being out of control. But don't all great spiritual teachings tell us that death is an illusion and that we're masters of our own universe? That we, and we alone, control our destiny? Many of us strive mightily for this goal. But we'll never get there if, under the water, we're back-pedaling like crazy out of fear we're going to lose control.

We need to learn to flexibly adjust, and to loosen our grip on things. We must learn to dance between steering our own ship through the rivers of life and being able to let go of the wheel. It's a fine balance. And the more we fear letting go, the greater will be our inner imbalance. With our soul movements out of sync, we'll lose any hope of controlling our final destiny.

So then what do we do? We grab for pseudo-control. But this of course adds more tension and anxiety to the pot. It scuttles any chance we had at peace and tanks our self-confidence, torpedoing our confidence in life in the process. The only way out—the way for real confidence to grow—is to give ourselves over to the unknown. We have to give up our tight holding on. If we will do this—if we will let go—we will discover something wonderful: full mastery of life without any fear of losing control. In short, we'll finally understand that there was never anything to fear.

To be fair, the typical person isn't yet capable of having total, immediate control of themselves or their lives. We still have to accept, at least for a time, that we have limitations. And these limitations within ourselves are going to create an undesirable destiny for us. Denying that this is the case—that we have limitations due to our own not-yet-healed imperfections—is a sure sign that we still have fear. And our denial, coming from our outer will, is only going to make matters worse.

To accept, on the other hand, our temporary limitations and their associated consequences, doesn't mean we resign ourselves to a life of tragedy and suffering. No, acceptance simply means we realize we're going through a rough patch that's uncomfortable, and we're willing to take responsibility for this state. Sure, there won't be much expanding going on for a time, and bliss won't be happening, but we don't need to dread this. This too shall pass. An attitude like this is what will open the door further, rather than slam it shut and leave us in the dark.

Our aim is to be in control of our own destiny. And if the potential to give over and trust the greater forces of life didn't exist somewhere inside us, we could never get there. We can at least trust that such a potential exists in us. This is a place to start. For in the end, it's our fear and distrust that causes us to hang on, refusing to relinquish control. And this is what's blocking us from freedom and bliss: our own fear and distrust.

Reaching Our Destiny

Another aim of ours is for pleasure. This is deeply inborn in us, just as our desire for control over our own life is embedded in our human instincts. Our psyche knows instinctively that both of these are our birthright. They are both our destiny and our origin, and we want them back.

But here's the thing. If we desire pleasure because we want to run away from pain, pleasure will elude us. But the absence of pleasure is not some big abyss of darkness, and so we don't need to shrink away from it. If we can understand this, we won't let our fear of pain steer us in the wrong direction.

This principle guides every aspect of living:

- If we fear being sick, we prevent being healthy.
- If we fear growing old, we prevent eternal youth.
- If we fear poverty, we prevent abundance.
- If we fear loneliness, we prevent true companionship.
- If we fear companionship, we prevent self-containment.

We could keep going. In every instance, the great enemy is fear. And the best way to conquer this formidable opponent is to start by admitting it's there. Just giving it voice will take a lot of the wind out of its sails. Articulating our fears will also open new doors for ousting this unpleasant guest.

It's always important that we formulate our desires, expressing them clearly in our thoughts and our intentions. This is going to be difficult, though, if we let our fear of our fear take us down. So calm admission and a willingness to accept, for now, that this is what's here will carry us further in eliminating our fears than trying to fight them.

Recall that the three main stumbling blocks in any human soul are pride, self-will and fear. But the more unified we become, the better we'll be able to reach the place in any inner division where things come together. Like with this triad, for example. Once we rid ourselves of fear, it will become quite easy to get past our pride and self-will. When we're no longer afraid of having our dignity pulled out from under us, we won't keep standing on the unstable ground of false pride. And once we're no longer afraid that either life or someone else is going to try to control us, we'll readily let go of our self-will.

Fear is the great locked door. It's what stops us from having access to all that could be available to us—right here, right now—the minute we uproot our fear from our heart and from our soul.

When it comes down to it, friends, this is the name of the game. This right here is what this whole school of life, with all its many repeated incarnations, is all about. And it's what this spiritual path is trying to teach us: fear is unnecessary.

Often, we hear the message but we get the meaning wrong. For instance, when we're told that we must learn to accept, we think we must accept that life is one long road of deprivation and suffering. When we hear that we must learn to let go of control, we think this means we have to release ourselves into a giant abyss of pain and hardship. Such misconceptions only increase our fear, and inflame our stubbornness and tense reluctance. We become more rigid, shrinking from freedom and pleasure.

But what's the truth of the matter? Acceptance must help us see that we are called to have whatever we most desire. Giving up control of our little ego-bound self-will, in the end, will show us that we can release ourselves into a new freedom, into something that's what we truly want. So there's no need to keep fearfully holding on.

Passing through Fear

When we finally become convinced of this truth that there is nothing to fear, acceptance won't seem like such a big deal. For it's not really a risk to accept and embrace the whole universe once we realize that it's perfectly safe. At that point, it will no longer be about going through fear in order to rise above it. Then we will be prepared to enjoy all the fulfillment and abundance, pleasure and bliss that living an eternal life of freedom entails. When we get past our fears, then everything our little human heart desires can be ours.

This truth is what our spirit has been waiting for. For this is the truth that will set us free. And when we see it—can truly take it in—it will be like: "How did I not see this before? Why did I put myself through so much unnecessary hardship?" And then we'll walk right out of the prison we've been living in. The world will now be ours.

If we're not ready yet, then we still need to learn some things. Like, that really, there's nothing to fear. But the only way to learn this lesson is by living in a world full of ignorance. It's by involving ourselves in this ignorance—by ignoring the truth that there is nothing to fear—that we will break through the clouds. We need to discover this truth for ourselves: Even what hurts is never quite what we fear.

For haven't we all had the experience of anticipating some particular event, and then, after we went through it, we realized it wasn't half as bad as we feared it would be? This experience offers us an important fact. The worst part of fear—it's main attraction—isn't the undesirable thing we fear itself, but the unknown quality of it.

Now, for sure, it's possible to fear something we've already experienced. But whenever we experience something while in a state of fear, all our faculties have been dulled. The truth of the experience, then, can't fully be perceived or digested. Our fear is going to blur our view of things so we can't evaluate the situation objectively. So it's entirely possible to go through a difficult experience in such a fearful frame of mind that we come out the other side thinking the experience was somehow different from what actually happened. Our perception will be that it was how we had expected it to be, not how it was.

This is why our souls need so many repetitions before we get it right and can rid ourselves of fear. This is especially true regarding the experience of dying. We can rest assured that the trauma of being born is infinitely harder than the one of dying. Still, we collectively believe that dying is way worse, for this is what is already imprinted in our souls each time we arrive.

So when it's time for us to transition out of this dimension, passing through the liberating event of releasing ourselves from our human bodies, this widespread belief will kick in and produce such fear that we'll be too anxious to register what really takes place. We won't be able to die with full consciousness and appreciate the event as it happens.

So instead of meeting this unknown element and experiencing the true facts of the dying process, our smart little brains become half-anesthetized by fear and our perception becomes warped. This is why the truth can't impress itself on our soul substance. Instead we end up with a hazy recollection. What's more, the fragments that do register are quickly forgotten, for our memories rely on a free state of mind that's not cluttered and fogged over by fear and misconceptions. What little we do remember is soon blotted out by the overwhelming power of that collective belief.

Frequently a dying person will register something like, "Oh my, is this what dying really is? How fantastic!" But in order for this to become the prevailing memory for this person, they will need to have been fully conscious at the time of their transition. If there's fear, then it's not possible to be fully conscious. But every time we pass through this sphere, there's an opportunity for a little more truth to land. Eventually, we'll be as relaxed about going through this transition as we are about going to sleep at night or about starting a new and as yet unknown phase in life.

Dying is produced by our fear of dying. When the fear vanishes, going through such things becomes superfluous, and it will therefore no longer need to take place. Then we'll be done with these cycles of incarnating.

Drawn to Duality

Earth is a dualistic sphere in which we must go through this experience of death. Thankfully, it's the only one. After this, we move onto other spheres where there will be other experiences that will be equally important for the evolution of our souls. But this is the only sphere that requires us to seemingly die.

What exactly do we mean by a "sphere?" We're talking here about a sphere of consciousness. In such a sphere, entities with a similar state of consciousness flock together, following immutable spiritual laws. Their overall state of development or consciousness can be collectively referred to as a sphere.

We're all familiar with looking at a geographical area or material space, like a planet, from such a point of view. But from a spiritual point of view, time, space and movement are all expressions of one particular state of consciousness. Our three-dimensional minds are challenged to imagine a consciousness that has other dimensions, and that also unifies all these different dimensions into a singular, greater consciousness.

So when we talk about spiritual spheres, it's quite possible that our minds will oversimplify them into terms of geographical areas that are located out there somewhere, in outer space. Yet it's not, in some way, untrue that the whole physical universe with all its many spheres lives within the self. And just as each planet is a reality that exists both within and without, many other spiritual worlds or spheres exist, both within and without. This is very difficult for us to comprehend.

When we are talking about the beings who inhabit these spheres, saying they have a comparable level of overall development, we need to not take this too literally. For surely we can look around and see that there are considerable differences in the development level of people. And this is also true among those in the other spheres of consciousness. But despite their differences—with older, more developed spirits capable of perceiving and understanding more than younger spirits—they all have certain points in common. And it's due to their similarities that they all can benefit by flocking together. This is why we've all been drawn together to make up this sphere on planet Earth.

To help visualize this better, consider that the conditions on Earth are a precise expression of the sum of the consciousnesses of everyone living here, plus of the individuals who aren't incarnated right now but will be coming back again. All the beauty we see in nature and that has been created by women and men is an expression of our inner qualities that are in harmony with the universe. By the same token, all the strife we see—including poverty and wars, sickness and dying—are an expression of our confusions and the destructive emotions we are clinging to.

So all our conditions, whether great or petty, favorable or unfavorable, are a direct result of the people who come here. And we can call all of this a sphere of consciousness. If, in another sphere, the overall level of consciousness is higher than here, conditions there will be more harmonious and less difficult. In a sphere where the spirits inhabiting it can perceive a higher level of truth, it's unavoidable that the circumstances in that sphere will be less limiting.

Great, so how soon can we go there? Well, until we have learned how to overcome the errors and disharmony we're facing here, we'll have to keep coming back to this sphere. Until we are capable of perceiving a higher level of truth, we just can't get there from here. For our outer environment and our inner state of consciousness must be a match. It can't be otherwise.

We're not "sent" here. No one "commanded" us to come here. It's a simple process of attraction and repulsion that follows spiritual laws. These laws work exactly the same as the laws of chemical bonds. So it's not correct to think that first a sphere exists, and then we are placed into it. It works the other way around. A sphere results from our thinking, our feeling, and our attitudes; it arises from the sum total of who we all are.

As such, our sphere expresses us. If we were to start expressing different qualities—like compassion, forgiveness, generosity and the like—we would no longer be drawn to this sphere, but instead we'd get to go to where the majority of beings are also expressing those qualities. But for now, we're all here.

Transcending Duality

In our minds, we human beings tend to draw an arbitrary hard and fast line between the physical and non-physical. But we humans are made up of lots of layers, and each layer is comprised of matter that has its own unique density. So then the higher the consciousness of a being, the finer will be the consistency of the matter that being is made up of. But that doesn't mean such a being lacks form or is any less real than a human being.

It's our beliefs that draw us to a sphere like Earth where matter is more physical, or dense. Other spheres have a finer vibration. If our entire thinking is geared toward being very superficial and materialistic, bringing us to this plane, the matter we produce for our vehicle—our body—will vibrate accordingly. In other words, the more ignorance we hold onto, with our errors, misconceptions, prejudices, limitations and darkness, the denser will be our matter, and the greater will be our suffering.

When it dawns on us that our Real Self is more than just our body, our perception of things widens. This shift allows the matter of our whole being—our entire soul—to become much finer and therefore more sensitive to the truth. We'll have a greater sense of reality.

And so it's super important that as we go along on our spiritual path, we find where we fear something negative, causing us to grasp for something positive. When we find these pockets of fear, and we see how we have a negative motivation for wanting something positive, we'll hold the key in our hand for setting ourselves free from this dualistic dimension.

Having the realization, "I am not able to step into freedom because I don't want freedom for itself, I want it because I fear being imprisoned," will bring us closer to liberation. Then, with our heads held high, we'll be able to accept all the rich abundance of life, as a free human being. It's this very soul movement that makes all the difference in the world.

As we've already discussed, it's our fear of death that gets us a return ticket to this particular sphere. But if we're afraid of dying, there must be other miscellaneous errors in our soul as well. Because everything is interconnected. Any time we have a fear that constricts us, we aren't going to be capable of merging with the cosmic stream of life that wants to wrap us in its arms and carry us along for a gentle, glorious ride.

In our tight holding, we will struggle against this cosmic force like it's our enemy. But the only enemy here is sitting inside us. And this enemy only exists because of our false fears, our wrong conclusions about life, and the limits we unnecessarily create for ourselves. Its these limitations that cause us to turn around and attack ourselves, in spite of the part of ourselves that wants to claim our birthright and become fulfilled. This other part is actually striving to go in the other direction, heading directly toward pain and misery.

We falsely believe that it's impossible to avoid some great danger, and somehow it seems less threatening to just quickly bring it about ourselves. At least then, we think, the "great danger" will no longer be unknown. But chomping down on an entirely avoidable negative experience is going to have a very bitter taste. For any time we court a negative experience out of fear and error, it will be much harder to bear than if such a negative experience surfaced organically due to our still lingering limitations.

It makes no sense for us to rush into danger voluntarily. But it may be very hard to see that we are doing this. For it takes deep insight into the mechanics of how our inner world operates to discover this mechanism at play. Only through such insight, though, will it be possible to stop repeating this destructive game.

There is a natural rhythm to our lives that we must learn to stop disturbing by struggling against, rushing into or forging blindly ahead. Then we can blend in with the great cosmic powers with which we can create. By guiding these powers using all of our conscious selves, we truly can become masters of the universe.

"Blessings for every one of you, my friends. May these words lift your spirit and bring you nearer to the light of truth, to the reality of love, to the unending bliss of spiritual existence. Be in peace, be in God!"

–The Pathwork Guide

Chapter 5

Giving up our Fear-Filled Struggle to Guard our Secrets

Our greatest joy in life comes from giving, to whatever extent we are able. It comes from reaching our potential, we might say. On the flip side, our greatest pain is derived from not meeting our full potential in giving to others and to life. Every other pain and frustration cascades from this pain of not offering up what we have to give. Turning this around, all pleasure and satisfaction flows from giving freely, no ifs, ands or buts.

Why then are we so stingy? Why do we refuse to give freely of ourselves? This stems from our fear of the parts of ourselves we don't yet see and know, which creates patterns that keep chunking out pain.

And for as long as we keep those parts hidden, we won't be free. We'll become a pretender who is always on guard. This means that wherever we are harboring distortions inside, we are living a lie. And none of this needs to happen. It's a needless lie we're living based on a false fear of own selves.

Some people, when they start doing this work of self-knowing, meet their private, hidden parts quite quickly. They dial them up, agree to have a chat, and directly go on to overcome their fears, walking out into the world a free person. But others, even some who have the best outer intentions to find themselves, skirt around the issue and get nowhere. They have this vague hope they can get all the way home without having to expose and clean up every last bit of inner dirty laundry.

The question is, are we ready to stop living the "big lie?" Are we ready to let go of all this pretense? It's a tough choice. It's a battle really, and it matters a lot if we win this one. To this end, let's look at where this illusory fear of the self comes from, and just as importantly, let's find out what happens if, instead of overcoming it, we coddle it.

Self-Alienation

There's only one way things are going to end if we keep on fearing ourselves: self-alienation. And this is going to flat out rob us of our birthright to be happy, joyous and free because it's going to short-circuit our giving and receiving mojo. For as our natural inner processes get dumped on their heads, we lose contact with our innermost self. On top of that, the inner mechanism that couples relaxation with independence goes haywire, derailing our capacity to build a realistic yet rewarding life.

Because we're now alienated from ourselves, we can't see how cause and effect is working, but we still refuse to reveal what's going on in there. So instead of truly finding ourselves, we find ourselves stuck at a crossroads, confronted with one good alternative, and one bad. Here's what's happening.

When we fear ourselves, it's because in some sort of way, we can't be what we want to be. What we want is to be ideal, which we then pretend to become. To be ideal is the apparently "good" option, but it's unrealistic and unrealizable. By contrast, the "bad" alternative seems to be exactly who we actually are, in this moment.

There is a lot that's wrong here. For starters, our concept of our present self is not right. It's exaggerated and distorted, especially since we haven't even taken a clear look at ourselves yet. But the goal we set for ourselves, to become ideal, is equally warped. So we're aimed at something unrealistic, which is to be better than we can be in this moment, and meanwhile we see ourselves as being worse than we really are.

Here's the truth: What we judge in ourselves to be horribly, unforgivably bad won't appear that way once we bring it out into the open and connect the dots of cause and effect. In contrast, when we quit this inner lie, we'll get an eyeful of negative trends in ourselves and we'll see just how undesirable they really are. But our awareness of this new reality won't make us feel "less than."

We're only crushed by what we think we are when our perceptions of ourselves are so unrealistic. At the same time, if we look more closely into the way we idealize ourselves, it will often prove to be less desirable than we had been thinking. In the end, both of these alternatives leave us feeling flat and lifeless.

Our unwillingness to look at our whole self sets negative chain reactions rolling. The first link is that many other issues in life will turn into a narrow "either/or" choice. This is a problem, because as we saw, even the "good" choice doesn't turn out well. So choices become impossible to make.

The ideal we were shooting for, which has always been unrealistic, must of course become unattainable, and perhaps even undesirable. All of life, starting with ourselves, seems to cleave down the middle, dividing into a rigid, sterile good side and a flat, bad alternative. We're not going to love either option. Either way, we feel tension and distinctly unreal.

So after our self-alienation gets underway, the next link in the negative chain reaction is that all options go south. Both the good and bad alternatives now look equally undesirable. Any time we're faced with two distasteful choices, our sense of truth and beauty has gone sideways. Everything, even the most desirable aspects of life, turn sour. We become incredibly confused.

Desire and Fulfillment

Let's looks at the typical real-life example of desire and fulfillment. These are two separate aspects that merge in a healthy person who is not alienated from their Real Self. Such a free individual will feel no pang or conflict about either one. A self-alienated person, however, will experience them both as something negative.

When it's healthy, desire is about reaching for new possibilities and becoming fulfilled. In distortion, desire turns into frustration. So then desire and frustration will drop into the same slot in a person's psyche, meaning desire won't be welcomed one little bit. In a similar way, when fulfillment is distorted, it turns into stagnation, like a dead-end street. A self-alienated person then, ping pongs between frustration and stagnation. In other words, between a rock and hard place.

When we no longer fear the self, we'll no longer fear either desire or fulfillment. For then we'll know our desires can be fulfilled, and fulfillment is not an end, but just another new beginning. But if we become disconnected from our real selves, our outlook will be so tainted it won't seem that fulfillment of our desires is even conceivable, much less attainable.

When that's the case, we'll reject our healthy desires too, and withdraw from desiring anything at all. To make up for this lack, self-willed greed will rear its ugly little head, out of our conviction that if we want to have anything, we have to scrap for it. Fulfillment, we think, is a pipe dream. And desire? Forget it.

To recap, when we are not willing to meet ourselves openly and freely— even the hidden parts we don't yet know—we also can't desire openly and freely. Frustration, then, is inevitable. But wait, isn't it true that sometimes we experience at least partial fulfillment, even though we're not yet clean as a whistle? Why then does it always seem that our fulfillment tarnishes and turns into stagnation?

This happens because fulfillment can only remain vibrant when our inner being is open and free. Then the cosmic river runs clear and clean, and pleasure is abundant. But when the spigot is even partially closed, things start to freeze up. Our soul becomes rigid and those free-flowing vital energies can't reach our core.

We then experience the self as finite rather than infinite, so every activity must come to an end. But this is not a happy ending, it's a flat thump that feels like a burden. We feel like everything is futile, creating a confusing feeling: "What is any of this for?" After all, why bother if even fulfilled desires are going to turn sour.

For a person who is able to be open and honest with themselves, fulfillment will be an unending, deeply satisfying continuum. What's to fear about that? But in distortion, we'll fear desire, regardless of how things turn out. If it goes unfulfilled, we fear it because the frustration stings. And if it is fulfilled, we fear it because we won't know what to do with it. All told, our fear of desire and frustration will be in direct measure to our fear of our own hidden self.

Only when we are no longer alienated from our self, will life be a vibrant experience where desire doesn't hurt, so desire and fulfillment can become one. Just as we will become one with our self.

Gaining Control

There's another chain reaction that self-alienation sets into motion: We get lost in the illusion we're not in charge of what happens within ourselves. We believe we're powerless over our feelings, our attitudes, even our thoughts and our actions. We fear that our negative emotions are going to control us and we won't have anything to say about it.

We ignore the fact that no thought or act can happen that we don't allow. But we lose ourselves in the illusion that we're not the ones running the show. "I feel such and such!" we exclaim, as though some feeling makes it impossible to find our way out of our unpleasantness. What we're overlooking is the simple fact that we determine our thoughts, our feelings and our actions. We're even in charge of how we *want* to feel and react.

If we are fully meeting ourselves, this self-determination will be for real. We won't be kidding ourselves about how we feel. And since we will know what we're really feeling, we can desire to feel differently and go in that direction. Such a desire is not nothing. It will have an effect. And we don't have to wait around to see what will show up.

Right away, we can make the choice to give in to our resistance and act destructively, or we can meet ourselves and determine a better course. It's an illusion that we have to go on feeling like we want to punch a wall or say something cruel until something other than ourselves unlocks the door and sets us free.

We're the ones who hold the key. We can instantly release our destructiveness by desiring something more constructive at this particular moment. But to arrive at a constructive desire, we'll need to know who and what we are. We'll need to know what's tucked away in the hidden chambers of our psyche. As long as we keep some destructive part of ourselves secret and separate though, masked behind our hazy and vague inner screens, we won't be able to know what a relevant constructive desire even looks like.

Let's say we take a peek and we find hate or hostility tucked away in there. Oh dear. What kind of effect might that have on us or our actions? We can say to our fear, "I am going to face my destructive feelings head on. This doesn't force me into actions. I am, after all, master of my feelings. I get to decide what my actions will be. I determine what I think, do and feel. I am ready to see what's in me. It is my desire to transform whatever I find into something truthful and constructive.

"If I discover something destructive that I don't want to give up, I don't need to deny that this is how I feel right now. I also don't need to give in to it. I can just greet this part of me. It's not the end of the world if I don't particularly like it. I also know that if this part is not in harmony with me, it's not in truth. I want to know the truth, and to choose more constructive ways of being in the world."

Taking an approach like this is the first step in coming back from self-alienation. It's the way to achieve self-government that is both relaxed and in truth. We don't need to strain or put on a false face. And we don't need to wait for permission to adopt such a stance. We can do it right now.

It's time to give up this notion that we can't help how we feel, or we're not responsible for our bad behavior. That's simply not the case. And don't forget, our actions include our attitudes, like the one that wants to let our resistance or negativity have free rein. "But this is the way I feel," we say, and put a period at the end like it's a done deal and there's nothing to be done about it. Friends, a miracle is not going to descend on us from outside and take away our troubles.

What escapes us is that we must first want to feel differently before we can free ourselves from the trap we're in. And what if we don't want to feel differently? Know *that*, and stop deceiving yourself. We can stop with the pretenses already, pretending we want to change but cannot. Once we know that, son of a gun, we don't *want* to feel differently, we can start to question why. Why do I want to stay in a negative, unpleasant state?

Keeping Secrets

When we deny the truth, which is that we're the ones who can choose how we think and behave, we give up one of the greatest powers we have available to us: self-government. Don't be confused. This is not the same thing as the false control we administer over our inner guards whose job it is to keep our secret parts hidden. Too often, we dump all the energy at our disposal into controlling our secret self. When we misuse our energy this way, we don't have any left for the part that could be working on creating a better life.

This notion that we must keep a part of ourselves secret comes from not believing in ourselves—in all of ourselves. Yet, as long as we shy away from exposing these parts that we fear, we won't be able to convince ourselves that underneath our distortions and destructiveness, our essence is utterly wise, totally trustworthy and seriously good. For if we were able to believe this, we'd realize there is nothing to fear.

We fear there's nothing reliable or rich at our core. We're suspicious that our inner being is not a creamy, nougat center that can nourish us. We're worried that the ultimate in us is that part that hates; it's that part that nurses destructive wishes and bad desires. We start out thinking we're only going to hide this from others, but then get lost in the game and hide it also from ourselves. That's how we lose touch with ourselves.

This work of becoming totally honest with ourselves is serious business. We must be willing to meet ourselves *where we currently are*. Then we can move on to discovering the ultimate in us, which we won't have to hide. Which we won't want to hide. But as long as part of us is in hiding, we're living by proxy. All our goals, as well as our fulfillments, are make-believe, never whole and real.

We could fear nothing if we didn't fear the part of ourselves we're keeping secret, even half so from our own selves. Before we knew it, we started pretending we don't believe this part even exists. This is the lie of our life. Even if it's only a little lie, it pervades everything so that somehow everything seems like a lie—even the stuff we are truthful about.

Here's the big promise: If, every day, we will state and restate our desire to, above all else, give up our inner secrets, we will meet the whole of ourselves. If we do this day in and day out—and really mean it—we cannot feel lost, stagnant or in disharmony with ourselves or others anymore. Our anxiety will slip away, along with feeling befuddled and bitterly hurt.

The procedure is pretty straightforward. We need to meet the whole of ourselves without any more hiding. It's time to stop allowing ourselves to be ruled by our unreasonable defenses that are effectively keeping us from knowing the whole truth inside. We must watch for our clever evasions. Notice how busy we get with other issues that have nothing to do with this. We need to take hold of ourselves instead of letting ourselves be controlled by our negativity, which snowballs into fear and then guilt and feeling helpless. It's up to us to change.

The world is such a wide place, with so many possibilities available to us when we stop keeping a tight check on ourselves. In the wider life, beyond our hiding, there are not just two alternatives, where one is falsely good and the other falsely bad. Nor are there only two bad options. In our new reality there can be many beautiful alternatives. In the greater reality, we can have all good.

Making Miracles

Meditation can be a valuable tool for bringing about the kind of miraculous changes we've been talking about. But what exactly do we mean by "miracle?" It's basically a law of life that we've only just now discovered. The law works like this: Whatever concept we hold—whether conscious or unconscious—must manifest in our life.

The truth of life, in this new reality that's free from illusion, is unlimited goodness. To the extent we can embrace this possibility—even if we're still holding an attitude of honest questioning about it—to that extent it must unfold for us, in whatever area we wish to apply it. When such goodness then unfolds, it seems miraculous to someone who was mired in negativity before.

Our expectations of life act like fences. When we discover greater possibilities, the fences recede accordingly. The greater our ability to grasp the possibilities for joy and bliss, the more of it must come into being. For in reality, it's all there, available in unimaginable abundance. Our narrow fences come from the distorted, untrue ideas in our minds.

We can't experience more than we can conceive of. So if we believe deep down that it's not possible to be happy, guess what: We won't be happy. This follows the same kind of logic as any physical law. So let's envision that we move our body from here to there. Now our body can only be in the spot we move it to; it can't be somewhere else. This isn't any more or less miraculous than what we can do with our minds.

As far as we can move our body, that's where we will find ourselves with it. If we find ourselves in a gloomy, narrow little room, we don't have to stay there. But we can't convince ourselves of this unless we walk out into the sunshine and discover there are much nicer places to hang out. If we resist any attempt to help us leave, maybe on the grounds that there isn't another room or enough space for us, we can't come out.

Regardless how long we want to argue about it, the only way to move is to actually make the move. If our limbs are healthy, this miracle awaits us. If we've let our limbs atrophy, we may need some treatment and exercise first to heal.

It works the same way with our minds. When we find out that another room beyond the one we're in actually exists, it will seem like a miracle to us. But we'll have to make an effort to go there. So often we remain stuck in a mental hole, when we could stretch and discover a beautiful world that's safe and satisfying outside our cramped little space.

This is what we must do with our psyche if it's lived for too long in a climate of negativity and isolation, after our misguided fears have limited us so much. But once we give up this limitation, the miracle must happen. It's a logical law that works for each and every creature in the universe.

The reality of creation is that our freedom is unbounded and there is every possibility for experiencing goodness. No one gets left out on this. But we might have to heal the "limbs" of our psyche to take advantage of what's available. If we keep frantically struggling to guard our secrets though, we can't experience the wide-open possibilities of life.

This struggle is a useless pain that we keep inflicting upon ourselves and that we can be rid of, starting today, if we so desire. But to do that, we must face the area we most fear and have been unwilling to see. That's where we need to shine our light and where we will feel the most reward. The freedom and safety that will follow is beyond words. These are not empty promises, friends.

"Be in peace, know how wonderful is the peace of truth by not shirking this truth. Be in God!"

–The Pathwork Guide

Chapter 6

The Painful Predicament of Both Desiring and Fearing Closeness

Our biggest struggle in life is the push and pull we face between our desire to overcome our loneliness and isolation, and our simultaneous fear of having close, intimate contact with another person. Often these are equally strong, tearing us apart from the inside and creating a tremendous strain.

The pain of feeling isolated always pushes us to try to escape from it by becoming more close with someone. Should such attempts appear to be getting somewhere, our fear of closeness will erupt and cause us to pull back again, and push the other away. And so the cycle goes with people, first erecting uncrossable barriers between ourselves and others, and then knocking them back down.

If we're walking on a spiritual path of self-realization, sooner or later we'll see the predicament we're in. For every disharmony, disturbance and shred of suffering we uncover has the same simple common denominator: our struggle between desiring and fearing closeness. And it's our insistence to holding onto both of these feelings that creates the barriers that keep us in separation.

Our relationships with other people will only go well when we are motivated by our innermost selves. For our intellect and will alone can't navigate the delicate balance of allowing our own self-expression while also receiving the self-expression of others. There isn't any rule that can be made to manage the rhythm of mutual exchange. And our outer brains are out of their league here.

The ego-mind is also not equipped to negotiate the fine balance needed between asserting ourselves and allowing another to assert themselves, between giving and receiving, between being active and being passive. And there are no pat formulas we can lean on. This doesn't mean our outer intellect has no value. It's an instrument that thinks mechanically, makes decisions, and determines rules and laws. But by itself, it doesn't have the intuitive sense or flexibility needed to meet each moment as it comes. It doesn't have the capacity to respond adequately. For that, we need to tap into the core of our being and activate our inner command center that's dynamically responsive. Then and only then can our relationship with someone else be spontaneous and satisfying for both of us.

If we're not in contact with our core, we won't be able to function right when life calls for a creative solution. We also won't be able to reach the inner center of another person. And this is precisely what needs to happen if we want to move out of isolation. For this is what *real* closeness and *real* relating are like, where intimate self-expressions flow with the stream of life and carry us to a place of vibrant peace. Anything short of that feels like effort, strain and difficult discipline, and none of these can ring the bell of reaching the joy of intimacy.

As we may have already figured out, people are terrified of themselves. We'll do everything we can to avoid having to look at ourselves. And yet, when we manage to move past some specific difficulty and resistance, we come to find that our fears weren't justified; we feel relieved and have a renewed sense of aliveness. Just then, at that moment, we've contacted our innermost self. But if we continue to evade ourselves—and our evasions can take many forms—it will be impossible to enjoy real contact with others.

Why do we have so much fear about contacting our own core or the core of someone else? It stems from our deep-seated refusal to give ourselves over to life. Believe it or not, this is our aim, to hold ourselves back, which is entirely destructive. Truth is, if we were willing to give our best to life, we'd never be in conflict. But instead we all sit on a pile of inner riches and won't offer them to life. Often, we're not completely sure what our assets are. Although even if we do sense them, it doesn't occur to us to offer them up.

However, once we open the tap of our inner wealth, something must start to happen. A great inner machine will spring to life that we have no reason to fear. An inner movement will begin to take place that operates in beautiful order and harmony. Each of us can move from being an isolated creature who keeps their assets to themselves, sometimes letting them lie abandoned and unused, to becoming someone who gives their best to life. The change such a shift can create will be so drastic, it's hard to convey it in words.

What before was bleak and laborious, filled with fear and strain and loneliness, will become easy and safe, relaxed and bright, and delightfully self-perpetuating. Things will fall into place automatically. We'll come to know a deep feeling of oneness with the world.

But until such a shift takes place, we'll feel perpetually caught in a whirlpool of wanting and fearing the same thing. And this, friends, is what torture feels like.

Two Necessary Approaches

This struggle of wanting and fearing closeness—both with others and with ourselves—can't be settled by deciding with our minds to give up one of the two alternatives: closeness or separateness. It doesn't work that way. The only way out is to surrender our destructive aims. Then the best of who we are will come tumbling forth. And then we will see that the only thing we have to fear is our own destructiveness. Give up this destructiveness and find the key to life.

It will help if we can devote a few minutes a day to thoughts like this:

"Whatever I am already, I want to give to life. I want to make the best use of who I am and what I have to give. I do not know yet what this even means, and what I do know may not be quite right. I am open to allowing greater wisdom to arise from deep within me and to guide me.

I will leave it to life to decide what a fruitful exchange would look like. For whatever I give to life, came from life. I want to return my gifts to the great cosmic pool so they can be shared with others and bring benefits to them. I know that this, in turn, will also enrich my own life, to the same measure I am willing to give. For truly, life and I are one.

When I hold back from life, I withhold also from myself. When I hold back from others, I also withhold from myself. Whatever I am, whatever is in me, let it flow into life. Whatever more is still waiting to be discovered, I desire to put that also to constructive use. I want to enrich the world around me."

With this approach of deliberately pursuing thoughts like this, and deeply meaning them, our problems will disappear like fog in the sun. Pain will go away and solutions will appear, even to problems that previously seemed unsolvable. This is a promise.

If, on the other hand, we feel a tight inner no-current when we speak words like these, then we now know what's causing the pain we feel in our isolation and in our relating to others. And note, these two things operate as a team. To whatever degree we suffer from isolation, to that same degree we'll have problems in our relationships. Further, to the extent we resist pulling ourselves out of isolation, to that extent isolation will feel painful.

It's hard to visualize the potentials hidden inside when we are locked in painful seclusion. The key lies in following our desire to offer what we have to give. This is what releases the lock. So before we've even fully experienced the powers within, we can deliberately call on them. Just knowing they exist will activate them and allow us to use them constructively.

Our second approach will be to meet every situation with total honesty. It's not enough to look at situations superficially. For when we only pay shallow attention to ourselves, we're likely to overemphasize our secondary positive goals and overlook our more powerful destructive aims. We must pay attention to every aspect we notice so we can discover what our real attitude is.

For if everything's not going great for us, not everything in us is constructive. Where could we be more sincere? More fair? This will bring our outsides into alignment with our insides, allowing us to cultivate a deeper connection with the divine powers that are lying dormant.

We need both of these approaches if we hope to move the meter, for both have great value. Some might be tempted to only work on activating their hidden powers. Others might concentrate on meeting themselves fully so as to eliminate their destructiveness. To pursue only one approach is a half-measure that will lead to limited results.

It's really easy to overlook what's going on in there. We need to see our negativity, yes, but we also need to improve our awareness of our positive potentials. Lack of awareness leads to limited chance for success. But if we do both together, while also upping our desire to contribute to life in whatever way we can, we'll see a tremendous power come to life. By activating our inner being, peace, safety and wonderful aliveness are sure to follow.

Our Basic Error

We are under the mistaken impression that if we add to life, we'll deprive ourselves. This, as one can readily imagine, creates a barrier to wanting to give to life. Conversely, we are of the wrong belief that only by grabbing for what we want—being solely concerned with attaining our own little advantage—can we nourish ourselves. This, we think, is the way to do justice to our desires and pleasure.

Such ingrained ideas motivate us to behave the way we do. And then here comes trouble. And frustration. Because the falseness behind these convictions makes us act, think and feel in ways that are damaging to everyone, including ourselves. Since we're not aware of how powerful such a wrong conviction can be—heck, we're often not even aware it's a wrong conviction—we don't understand why our efforts aren't leading us to rewards. We become increasingly confused, setting off painful chain reactions whose nature we can't comprehend.

Here's the basic error: It's never me versus the other. Nothing could be further from the truth. It will be helpful if we can meditate on all the places this error shows up in our lives. Once we see how much this belief is playing out on the level of our ego, our goal is to try to comprehend, from another level of our being, how the opposite is true. For that's the truthful view.

Confront this mistaken concept of the ego with the deeper knowing that only by desiring to give to life—to add something to creation—can we experience pleasure. There is no pleasure we can think of that needs to be denied us. This will set the gears of our psyche going in a positive direction. We'll start moving in a constructive direction such that even the highest pleasure can and will manifest for us. We will activate our own selves, but not as a selfish move. We'll replace the incorrect "me versus the other" attitude, which leads to isolation, with "me and the other."

When our psyche becomes geared toward "me and the other," the apparent conflict between giving and receiving will disappear. We will no longer refuse to give to life. Deep sorrow and suffering, then, will also cease. Guilt and frustration will be no more. The terrible see-saw in which we suffer from isolation, reach out, succeed and then push people away, will end. Our struggle will be over.

On and on we've been doing this: We eliminate barriers because the pain of isolation has become unbearable, only to set up new barriers because we're overwhelmed by our fear of closeness. Where does this fear of closeness even come from? It comes from that wrong conviction that we have to save ourselves from being annihilated. But we only hold this perspective of life's malignant nature to whatever extent our own deepest aims are malignant.

Our work is to break down this vicious circle that pits us against life's malignancy, as though we need to do battle with life. And this can only be broken down by wanting to contribute generously to life. Then, and only then, will we find that life is safe. It's benign. Just like our innermost self. No more so and no less so.

Letting Go

As long as our psyche is geared to go in a negative direction, we'll fear intimate contact. Being in a relationship, then, will seem frightening. For who's it going to be: Me or the other? Who will win? And if it feels frightening to pursue our destructive aims—which it will—everything becomes dangerous. It's dangerous to explore ourselves, it's dangerous to make contact with someone, and it's especially dangerous to give ourselves up to the bliss of union.

That we must desperately avoid because it threatens to cost us our control. And without our control, our destructive tendencies could take over and threaten annihilation. So giving up control looks a lot like death. We'll be giving up our safety if we give up our self-will. This is what really goes on as long as we hang on to our destructive aims by offering them a safe haven in our psyche.

This is why it seems to the immature psyche that the only smart thing to do is to build barriers around the self. Only this will keep the self intact. The built-in tragedy here is that as long as we allow our destructive goals to go unchecked, isolation will be what gives us a sense of identity. It will seem like the best option for preserving our individuality.

But in fact, the only way that loss of control leads to death or loss of self-power is in this negative context. Ultimately, the endgame of this conflict is mental disturbance.

When we switch from believing in a "me versus other" world to "me and the other," and correspondingly desire to give who we are and what we have to life, we won't fear loss of control. Because letting go of ego control will actually lead to having more control, and in a healthier, fuller sense. A constructive psyche can be trusted to be spontaneous and free. It can give itself up to inner powers that get along very nicely with life. So we can flow with life and enjoy the unity of all that is.

When we ask the little ego to give up control, we get something even better in return. For we will be activating the constructive powers that live deep at the core of our soul. And those powers make us forever more capable of determining our own fate in the best possible way. We only need that tight inner gripping when our psyche is riddled with negativity. But such holding on prevents union and free self-expression. For joyful living can only happen in a relaxed state. See the problem?

Hoping to avoid a disaster, many people hold on with ever tightening control. The big danger is that we will eventually exhaust our psyche until it lets go in a long process of extended self-alienation. So now we can start to understand the paradox that giving up control will actually lead us to better control, whereas tightly holding on to control will eventually bring loss of control.

It's like this with all great spiritual truths: on the surface of things they seem contradictory. If we want to perceive the unity of these contradictions, we'll have to use our deep inner listening, and not just the outer ears linked directly to our brains. For our intellect can only take us so far. If we want to verify such statements, we'll have to live their truth. And this can only be done by following the steps of our spiritual path.

The threshold we must cross to move from self-alienation to harmony may seem daunting. But in truth, we make it harder than it needs to be. We stand there, wanting to leave our place of isolation and greed, where we demand the most from everyone else. But we fear people aren't going to comply with us and, in turn, are going to demand from us what seems dangerous to give. If we stay stuck, waffling in this doorway, we will indeed feel deeply troubled.

What's the way to the other side? We have to think deeply about this situation and these words, using more than our mental minds. We must consider the truth of "me and the other," and realize it's not true that we're safer if we keep pursuing negative aims, hoping to defeat everyone and their brother and sister. For that's not the road to glory. We must reach the point where our negative aims are staring us straight in the face.

It's only then that we will see how futile our struggle has been. It will become obvious that our approach hasn't been working and never will. We don't have to keep using our separating mechanisms, because what we are is good, and we don't need barriers and masks. We can begin to offer up our goodness and this new knowledge that it's safer to be wholly who we are will come.

The entire human struggle hinges on this mistaken belief in "me versus the other." When we start to digest this truth, this simple truth will set us free. We can make the first step toward liberty by meditating on these words:

"I am ready to give up this wrong notion that it's 'me versus the other.'

There really isn't a conflict, so I can give all of myself to life. I ask for help from deep inside, and decide to give my best, without fear. Any fear I am harboring is in error. I decide to rid myself of this error and open myself instead to the divine powers that are waiting to guide me.

"I want to see the truth that 'I am one with others,' which means there's no conflict between us. I surrender. I wish to allow higher forces to lead me to harmony, in rightness, without effort or strain."

If we meditate like this, we'll increase the light within. Our difficulties will disappear in exact proportion to our embracing of this attitude. We must feel and live this key to life, and then everything else will come. But superficial words won't turn things around.

The Common Denominator

Try applying this beautiful formula to a specific problem you are facing. For if we look closely, we'll see that every problem can be brought down to a simple common denominator: We fear giving of ourselves, and instead are feeding a destructive attitude. This is why we have the problem. The trouble is, our withholding and our belief in "me versus the other" set off negative chain reactions, and they really are damaging to us. This makes it look like our wrong conclusion that "it's me versus the other" was right. This snow-balls until our problems have turned into avalanches.

For many of us, we have the peculiar experience of creating positive self-perpetuating chain reactions in one part of life—where everything proceeds fairly easily—while in our problem areas, people and life respond in a totally opposite way. What we don't realize is that in these two areas, we have completely different responses to life.

It's our own outlook that's responsible for our "good luck" or "bad luck." We're the ones behind the curtain determining fulfillment or frustration. That's why it's so incredibly important that we take the time to figure out what we actually think and feel. Self-confrontation is our way through to the other side. Giving up our resistance is our key.

Good can't exist on its own, in isolation. That's just the nature of anything good. It has to communicate. It has to include others. Yet we fear offering our best, and this holding back creates tension and anxiety in us. From here, it appears safer to remain unproductive and barren. We feel uncomfortable receiving, but that's only because we fear giving of ourselves.

In this immature state, we have this childish, selfish aim to receive as much as we can and give as little as possible. This of course can never happen, not only because it's an unfair deal for everyone else, but because it doesn't correspond to truth and to spiritual law. And these laws can't be broken; they contain their own order.

It's a simple mathematical equation really: We will no longer feel cheated by life when we no longer cheat life by withholding from life. We can use this formula to our advantage. We should use it as much as we can. We should want to use it! It holds healing power for transforming a dull life into a dynamic one. It will lead us out of aloneness and into abundance in every respect. Test the truth of these words, friends, and life will reveal its limitless possibilities.

"Be in peace, be in yourself, in God!"
–The Pathwork Guide

Chapter 7

How Fear of Releasing the Little Ego Spoils Happiness

Underneath our ordinary, neurotic, unconscious wrong thinking lies a difficult conflict embedded in all of humanity: We have a deeply ingrained longing to be happy and, at the same time, we fear happiness. And this fear is directly related to our fear of letting go. By the same token, our longing to be happy must also be a longing to be released from the clutches of our little ego. The two are linked. Let's now dive into a deeper level of this topic so we can come to a new understanding.

Everything exists in both a right understanding and in distortion. Letting go of the outer ego is no exception. It's possible then to let go in an unbalanced, distorted manner, which is unhealthy. Now first, what are we talking about when we say "let go of the ego?" These are the faculties we have direct access to: our volitional thinking and our will that we have the power to direct.

Here's a simple example of the difference between direct will and indirect will on the level of the physical body. With our direct will, we can decide to move our hand, directing how it will move and what we're going to pick up with it. But for our heartbeat or circulation, we have no direct control. We can however regulate our heartbeat and circulation by controlling the movement of our body.

Our will also works the same way on the mental and emotional levels. We *do* have the ability to change unpleasant feelings, but it's futile to try to do this directly or quickly. What's more, when we direct our will in the wrong way, we can throw our psyche into a state of disarray.

When we overexert our will, then, by trying to exert it in areas it can't directly control, we waste energy and debilitate ourselves. It's the equivalent of throwing all our might into changing our heartrate using our sheer outer will. If this works at all, it only worsens our condition. In truth, we have lots of way to improve our circulation, but forcing—by using our outer will—isn't one of them.

We human beings do this a lot: We use the wrong approach. We force our will where it doesn't belong and then neglect using it where it could be doing a lot of good in our personal development. When we don't use enough will in the right way, our ego becomes weak. When we use too much, our ego becomes so exhausted it will try to escape from itself. Letting go like this, though—from weak motives instead of from a place of inner strength—is an escape that can become quite dangerous to the self.

The Healthy Ego

If we want to properly let go, we need to start with a healthy, balanced ego, not one filled with false ideas, false fears and destructive attitudes. This is the way to give up our over-tight direct control. Then letting go will not only be possible, but also desirable. All great human experiences arise from this releasing of our too-tight control to some degree, and deep down we all know this.

All creativity is a direct result of an inner wisdom and intelligence that far surpasses what's available to the ego-mind. So we want to use our conscious ego-intelligence to deliberately activate the greater wisdom within, which appears to have a mind of its own. And in a way, it does. At first, we're often completely unaware that such a powerful inner intelligence even exists. Then we start to experience it occasionally as this entity that's not even connected with our conscious selves. Finally, we will integrate these two parts of ourselves.

In order to accomplish this integration, we'll need to learn how to use our conscious ego for the purpose of waking up our inner self. To do this, we must also learn the fine balance between when to apply the gas and use our outer ego, and when to apply the brake and allow our ego to step aside.

All acts of creation, whether in the sciences or the arts, arise from the inner, non-volitional self, never from the outer ego alone. All great inventions, all lasting values, and all deep spiritual experiences come from the integrated inner self.

Misidentification

Strange as it sounds, humans fear having a great spiritual experience the same way we fear death, which we assume to be horrible. We've also exaggerated our fear of death so much we've turned it into a seemingly rational fear. Further, we fear the great act of love and the letting go of the little self during the ecstasy of union. In the end, we're afraid to muster the courage needed to let our inner selves manifest, bringing forth its wisdom and truth.

We are under the misconception that we can only maintain life when we hold it tightly together. That's why we're afraid to let go. In this sense, what does "life" mean? It means we don't want to lose our identity. We don't want to stop being an individual with a unique existence, a distinct life. Unfortunately, what we're usually thinking of as our identity is our outer ego's ability to direct our thinking and our will.

This misidentification causes us to fear losing ourselves. For who would we be without our volitional thoughts and actions? If we let go, we'll lose our ego and this means death, we think, because we'd feel nonexistent. Faced with "I am not," we'll keep holding on tightly, thank you, trying to hold ourselves together.

As humanity has evolved spiritually, we have arrived at this temporary state of holding on too tightly to our egos. Now it's time to learn to reestablish balance. In our more recent evolution, we've concentrated overly much on using our ego faculties alone, such that we can't see past the seemingly solid wall of matter in front of us. As the ego sees it, this wall separates us from life. This is why we associate our physical separateness with our individuality.

Yes, it's true that having a weak, ineffective ego diminishes our sense of ourselves as a person. Ironically, that's the reason we need to strengthen our egos: for the sole purpose of relaxing them again. Then we can integrate our ego selves with what's indirectly accessible, but which is deeper and wiser.

When we identify exclusively with our outer ego, we must fear letting it go. For doing so threatens our very existence; it seems like annihilation. Our separateness actually results from this threat. It's the very deepest root of our fear of letting go. But as long as we don't loosen this grip, we can't have true happiness.

For all truly beautiful and meaningful experiences emerge from a perfect balance between our volitional outer ego and our non-volitional inner self. Valid and constructive experiences will manifest spontaneously only as long as there's no overexertion from the ego. And these are the experiences that make us feel at one with the world.

The fact that we constantly long for this oneness—and regardless of whether we're aware of this longing, it's there—is totally understandable. For that's where we're all heading. It's our natural state. Evolution is pushing all of us in the direction of unity. This is where we have to go. But we can't get there if we're clinging to our ego, refusing to drop into connection and integration with our deeper selves.

When we unwittingly block ourselves from our destiny by trying to escape life and letting our fears and misconceptions lead to self-alienation, we create a conflict deep in our psyche. Then our greatest longing—to reach the fulfillment of oneness—becomes our deepest fear. This dichotomy between desire and fear will be strongest in the areas of our lives where our strict control won't allow our ego to step aside and let our inner self surface.

In the areas where such over-control has gone on for some time, we'll become exhausted. That's when we resort to false means for freeing ourselves. We can't stand how the burden of our too-tight control has overloaded our faculties and cut us off from our inner selves—which are infinitely better equipped to serve us—so we start looking for relief.

In an effort to experience the wonder and richness of the universe, we'll grab hold of whatever false means—even dangerous ones—will help us flee our over-functioning egos. There are myriad ways we unconsciously try to escape from ourselves. Alcoholism and drug-addiction are more extreme forms of what often arises; dissociating is a less extreme form. Then when these bring unpleasant results, we become all the more convinced of how dangerous it is to let go. So we fall back into the other extreme of holding on too tightly to the ego, which is what caused the imbalance in the first place.

Only a healthy, robust ego can afford to let go of itself. Such a strong ego can give itself up and mesh with the larger self. Letting go, then, is the story of the human ego that has a happy ending.

Self-Perpetuating Processes

When we consider the story of our life, we may find there are areas that function perfectly well. Perhaps we've arrived into this life functioning healthy and free in certain aspects. Or maybe we've done enough spiritual healing work in a particular area to have established healthy patterns. However we got there, the positive self-perpetuating principle is working.

All self-perpetuating processes are like magnetic fields, with new energy constantly arising from their nucleus. So every attitude we harbor about an area of our lives—made up of all our impressions and actions—forms a nucleus of energy that creates reactions and interactions. For each of us, a number of basic life experiences combine to form such force fields.

Some of the fundamental ones applying to all of us are: our attitude toward work, our relationships in general, our values about material things, our physical health, and our outer appearance and activities. A magnetic field is also created by our attitude toward nature, leisure, art and pleasure, and by our take on spiritual reality, self-development, and assimilating new information. These all form separate energy fields that attract.

In every human life, some of the self-perpetuating fields we generate will be positive and some will be negative. Where they're positive, things go smoothly. We don't struggle and yet desirable results come our way as if by themselves, without creating problems for us. There is effortlessness and harmony. We take the right action at the right time, both inwardly and outwardly. We say and do what's appropriate at just the right moment. Nothing stands in our way. Things fall into place.

We are guided by our own inspiration and resourcefulness, which function well. In such areas, we're apt to take smooth functioning for granted, unaware of the mechanics of what's happening behind the scenes. But if we start to pay attention, we'll see that our ego is doing its part, but it's not exclusively in charge. For it would be out of its league trying to get so many factors to function so well together. That's a typical description of a positively working magnetic field.

What's our life experience like when there's a negative magnetic field in operation? It's not just that there will be failure and difficulty, but there will also be pressure, wrong timing and frustration. Things won't work out. When we look more closely, we'll see that the ego is pushing, assuming that's what is needed to overcome the obstruction. What follows instead is pain and disappointment.

Sorry to report, it doesn't work to directly control the result itself. We waste our energy when we try, thinking we can change a negative field into a positive one. For that's not what we can control. We can, however, directly control all the things that make up a negative field.

That is to say, we can examine ourselves. We can uncover our hidden thoughts and feelings and attitudes. Once we're aware of them, we can decide if we want to continue in the same vein, or change. We're in charge. Would we rather stay stuck in a climate of helplessness and hopelessness, or are we willing to clean up our inner climate and subsequently create a new positive attitude? It's our call.

Unearthing Magnetic Fields

No one is more fatalistic than a person who is blinded by the material world, ignoring spiritual realities. Such people are often superstitious, believing in "good luck" and "bad luck" because they can't see what's going on beneath the surface of what's seen with their eyes. In our shortsightedness, we call the results of a positive energy field good luck, and the negative, bad luck. As a result, we overlook the fact that we have an influence on those unlucky areas.

But unlucky areas aren't going to change without honest self-confrontation. And this must start by realizing that it could be possible for change to happen. But we can't just press for change. We have to use our will to discover the nuts and bolts of our negative self-perpetuating machinery that we ourselves have created. We have to make the effort to reorient ourselves. Then we can set new positive fields into motion. That's the way to turn things around.

How do we find out if we have any destructive material inside generating negative force fields? It's quite simple: How do we feel about letting go of our ego control? If this brings up fear, we've got work to do. But hang on a second. If our destructiveness is being generated by a negative magnetic field that's egging it on, won't letting go of outer control amount to handing the reins to this out-of-control force? From this point of view, our refusal to let go is understandable. It might even seem like healthy self-protection.

In fact, when we become ready to use our volitional will to unearth the root of our problems in life, our fear of letting go is going to come up. It just is. So how do we keep this from overwhelming us? We need to get specific: "In what specific areas of my life are negative force fields operating?" We need to see them clearly, perhaps even writing them down. Be precise. But let's also be sure to see the positive fields. Put them side by side. This is important. None of us have only negative magnetic fields.

Seeing how both modes are operating will help us relax. For the negative parts are never all of us. That's what we fear to be true, but it's not. And those negative magnetic fields will already begin to weaken just by being looked at and understood. Positive self-perpetuation then is just around the corner.

When positive fields are working—whether we're conscious of them or not—there will be trust. The bigger our ratio of positive to negative fields in our psyche, the greater we'll trust in the natural flow of life. The more we trust, the more letting go won't be a problem. This is the only way to establish trust in life, trust in ourselves, and trust in God.

To tell someone to trust in a faraway God is a meaningless command that too often turns into an impossible demand. Rather, by correcting our negative fields that endlessly produce painful patterns, we'll discover that life—and therefore God—are trustworthy. By understanding how and why our negative fields work, and why they exist, it will become self-evident they don't need to exist. Then our trust will be justified, even before all our inner distortions have been transformed.

So underneath every negative magnetic field is something that can be trusted and activated. The more we contact this vast but now-hidden power, the easier it will be to switch over all our circuits, in all areas of our lives, converting destructive channels into constructive ones.

We must strengthen the muscles of our egos so they become strong and healthy. That's the only way to integrate ourselves with the utterly reliable part of ourselves that operates independently. We're not some passive bystander, waiting for things to happen *to* us. No, they need to happen *through* us. We have a role to play. Leaving ourselves out of this process is not any better than taking too much control of the reins. Just as we don't want to overburden our egos, we don't want to cast them aside.

Friends, we won't reach our destination—which is to activate the powerful inner being at the core of each one of us—by charging our egos with tasks they're not equipped to execute, or by escaping from ourselves and cutting off our possibility for inner connection. Indeed, it's only by activating our inner being that we can live in harmony with our egos. Then trust, relaxation and a wider world will come into being.

The self-discovery process outlined in the Pathwork teachings provides a map for doing this work of integration. It is a process of recognition, which may sound easy but is often quite hard to do. For we are wired to glibly rationalize away our impulses and drives, without pausing to understand their real nature. To recognize ourselves deeply is a long road that requires courage and a willingness to be honest. Without these things, we can't get there from here.

When we first attempt to observe ourselves closely, we might feel anxious; or we may find ourselves feeling impatient or irritated. Instead of explaining these feelings away, it helps to jot down some key words. Otherwise they will easily slip away. What are the moments exactly that make us feel uneasy? When has this happened before? What fleeting thought just went past when this anxiety came up? Try to pinpoint it. Hold onto it. After a period of days or weeks, a list of key words will form. From this, a clear pattern or common denominator will surface. This may be a comparatively easy way to sense a larger negative energy field that hasn't been evident before.

Our evasions cause us so much needless suffering. We feel fear arise and we run for an escape. By facing ourselves, though, relief and growth are possible. Perhaps we can see that what we fear is the truth. Then we can say to ourselves: "I don't need to fear the truth. This is not a rational fear. It's not founded in reality. It's illogical. I will not give in to this fear. I am making a decision to face whatever it is. I wish to know the truth and I ask for all the help available to do so."

Fear in Relationships

Let's say we're just starting into a new relationship and things look promising. How do we move forward knowing our still-existing problems may impede the relationship and ultimately ruin it? In truth, we don't. But think how much more likely it is that this could happen over and over, with us remaining blind to what's really going on, until we become so bitter we withdraw from life altogether.

Think how much more painful it is to blame false reasons, and how much more constructive life could be when we learn from everything we experience. For make no mistake, absolutely everyone destroys some chances as they go through life. After all, every single incarnated soul has some unresolved problems and blocks.

Also know this: We can't be drawn to anyone who doesn't have equal, complementary problems to ours. No more and no less. So both parties in any relationship are equally responsible when things don't work out. If we're under the wrong impression that others can't blunder, and if we feel guilty that we're not "like others," we'll feel overly anxious and compulsive.

But when we catch on that perfection doesn't exist here, and that everyone is just doing their best, wherever they are on their journey, then we can relax. What's important is that we accept ourselves where we are right now, with all our present limitations and the consequences they create. That's how to set about eliminating the limitation and getting more and more joy from each encounter.

Eventually, with each new contact, we'll become less afraid of people, of love, and of ourselves. Through our growing openness, we'll contribute more to others, which in turn will boost our own security. With such an attitude, we won't be living in illusion or distortion. We will see reality and we will grow from what we see. We can't expect to have all our blocks disappear in one fell swoop.

Let's not get caught thinking that on the other side of the fence are all the other human beings, and they have no problems, only fully functional relationships. Let's not be believing that no one else ever destroys anything, while we sit all alone on this side of the fence. Don't think that if only we could quickly get rid of all our blocks, we too would be standing over there among the privileged ones.

All people inadvertently destroy chances all the time. This is part of the human condition. But making mistakes is not the end of the world. If we learn nothing other than this, we will already stop being so frightened.

Every relationship we enter into is a mutual proposition. If it's not a good relationship, that's on all parties involved. Relationships are never a one-side affair. When we know this, we can take our power back. It's the immature, egocentric child in us that sees things as one-sided and only expects to receive. In a strange paradox, the weaker and more helpless such an egocentric person is, the more they tend to blame themselves alone when a relationship fails. For when we can only see our own needs and desires, we think we're the only ones who count. So then we can't share the brunt of failure when a relationship falls apart. At the same time, such a person can't access their inner power so they can be giving toward the other person.

On the other hand, when we become more mature, outgrowing our ego-centricity, we can experience ourselves as being on the same level as the other person. So then our concern for the other person must grow. We will realize that we also hold the power to make someone else happy or unhappy, which is something we had previously thought only the other person could do. This will make us feel much more secure.

As this shift occurs, it's likely we'll fluctuate between blaming ourselves and blaming the other person. Our goal is to not show up as a begging child, so we can know our own strength and our potential to give. Our intelligence, observation and intuition will all be important, as will our ability to balance both our active and passive contributions to the relationship.

How freeing it will be to realize that both people are involved. For if the other person had no problems, their healthy state would overcome all the difficulties in the relationship. That's the power of true spiritual health. Never forget that all negative fields can be reversed, if we truly desire this and are ready to do the work.

"Be blessed, my dearest ones. Be in peace. Be in God."
–The Pathwork Guide

Chapter 8

Three Things that Underpin Self-Fulfillment

To have self-fulfillment, we need to be in harmony with ourselves and with life. There are three topics that form the basis for achieving this harmony:

1) Having a positive concept of life that sees the universe as safe.
2) Being free and fearless to love.
3) Holding a healthy balance between the forces of activity and passivity.

Let's weave these together to see how they create one comprehensive whole. For they all depend on awakening our innermost self and activating the core that we can call the Real Self. Without that, it's our ego running the show. And as long as our ego is our sole motivator in life, it will be impossible to have confidence that life is safe. This will make it impossible to be fearless about loving. It will also make it impossible to find that delicate balance between being active and being passive. Let's take a closer look.

To have a healthy concept of life is to have a truthful concept of life, which is that life is utterly benign. Life is safe. When we stray from knowing this truth, we'll experience life as hostile and we'll feel the need to defend ourselves against it. On our spiritual path, as we dig through the layers of our psyche in an effort to untangle any disharmony, somehow we always find that we're sitting on a negative concept of life.

A negative concept of life is not a benign thing, because it interacts directly with our faults. And this interaction is a two-way street. First, we're driven by the destructive forces caused by our negative concept of life. This expands our negative beliefs, even if we're hardly aware of them. Second, our negative beliefs cause us to take a defensive posture toward life, and that perpetuates our destructiveness.

By examining our faults, we can begin to unwind all this. The first step, as is so often the case, will be to become aware of our faults. While not easy, this isn't that difficult if we approach the task in the right way. Once we have a list of our faults, the second step is to understand why they exist. Why do we cling to them? If we look closely, we'll see they are intended to ward off something bad we feared would happen to us. So they sit on the fixed foundation of a negative assumption we take for granted.

Having spotted this, we're ready for the third step. We need to question this assumption. Is it true? What would happen without this fault? No, seriously. Is it possible that this assumption is wrong? And how is this fault affecting others? For whether our faults are acted out or just thought about and felt, they have an effect.

Our goal is to expand our view of things and see the greater significance of the fault we're dealing with. For in order to truly want to rid ourselves of a fault, we have to comprehend how it affects others, and consider whether it's actually doing its job. When we are no longer sure it's really working to protect us, and when we are able to see that we are possibly being harmed by it, not helped, and when we also see that our fault is hurting others, then, and only then, will we want to put our energy into something more positive. We'll become ready to replace our habitual old fault with a new, constructive attitude.

If we want to transform our lives for the better, this is the way we must go. Almost never can we get there any other way. It's just not possible to transform something we aren't aware of. And it's impossible to transform some attitude we're holding onto if we don't know why we're holding onto it. We have to understand it and see how it's affecting people. We can't gloss over these things or hope that some vague recognition will be enough. Transformation can't happen in the face of such ignorance.

Know what else we're going to need? Our Real Self, which we can contact and activate with our egos. Without this access, we won't have the stamina to go the distance. This is the circuit that requires connecting to give us the light we need to see what's hiding in the dark.

Free and Fearless Loving

Now let's look at how being fearless is a precondition for loving. If we've been on a spiritual path for any length of time, we've probably seen the way fear of loving underpins most of our human predicaments. This may take different forms in different conflicts or with different people, as fear of loving can appear with many different guises.

But really, by now, the entire world has generally caught on to how important love is. Any truthful teaching will tell us that love means freedom and peace and life. Lack of love, then, equals conflict, enslavement and death. To be without love is to be restless, anxious and unhappy. Everyone is on the same page on this one, including psychologists and psychiatrists.

And still, people often find it so hard to give themselves fearlessly to this eternal stream that flows from deep within. Why is that? After all, our natural state of existence is to be loving. Yet we manage to cover that up and contort love into unnatural forms. These twists and turns keep us alienated from our own center, where love is a natural stream that flows with effortless ease. Love is a natural phenomenon that comes preinstalled in every human being. We hinder love only because we fear it.

Sadly, we often think we must be able to define love to have it. So we grope for these definitions with our minds, assuming that if we understand love intellectually, it might land in us. The error lies in believing love comes to us from the outside. In reality, love exists in its perfect form, right there in our core.

But if we really insist we need a definition of love, it would be this: Love is whatever furthers unity, inclusion and expansion; love is whatever allows the safety of the universe to unfold. Anything that ignores the beautiful, benign nature of life goes in the direction of exclusion and separateness, and that would be definition of the opposite of love.

The opposite of love could also be called the opposite of life, or nonlife. In other words, the opposite of love is some degree of death. For just as there are many degrees of life, there are many degrees of death. And yet here we are, fearing love, which means we fear the life, peace and freedom that only love can bring. Meanwhile, we cling to the separating forces of being non-loving, as though somehow that's going to protect us.

So let's not delude ourselves that we love, when there are places where we're refusing to reach out and connect. For anywhere we have problems, whether on the inside or the outside, there's a lack of love going on. For sure, this is almost never all of us, but it's always somewhere in all of us. It's useful, when we dredge up an awareness of where we refuse to love, that we compare this with the areas where we do love.

If we feel determined to not love, this resistance is always coupled with—caused by, actually—a fear to love. It's crucial that we start to make this connection and not skip or neglect this during our self-confrontation: "Here is where I do not love, and the reason I don't want to love is because I am afraid to love."

At this point, we don't yet know why. We might come up with some clichéd theories or glib answers. Like, "If I love, I'll be more vulnerable to being hurt." But is this really convincing? Think about it. Let's admit this isn't really true.

Perhaps we'll see that we enjoy indulging in vindictiveness. It feels good, we think, to strike out at others. This is probably closer to the point we need to find. It's good to uncover such feelings fully, accept them, and try to understand them. But this is still not the whole story. And we won't be able to sort this one out completely until we bring in the third topic.

Love and the Ego

But before we go there, let's circle back and realize this: It's impossible to transform our fear of love from our ego, just as it's impossible to transform a negative attitude or concept to a positive one using exclusively the ego. It just can't be done. This is so because the quality of love doesn't live in the ego, it resides in the Real Self. The ego has other functions, like discerning and taking action, but alas, it does not possess the faculty of love.

Love is a feeling that arises wholly from the inner self. That's why we can't understand love in terms of intellectual processes, as so many try to do. We can't conceptualize love because it's not a concept of the ego-mind. It's a feeling we must permit. And in order to give ourselves complete permission to love, we must realize our inner being and have a positive concept of life.

Now, if it were true that life is hostile and intent on depriving us, then it would indeed be dangerous to love. But if life is safe, free and giving—if life is *for* us and not *against* us—then not only is it safe to love, but loving is the only way possible to be at peace and live in harmony with the world.

So then it's critical we connect our fear of loving with our negative concept of life. Which means we can have freedom from fear of loving if we adopt a positive concept of life. Even if we are in total harmony in certain areas of our lives, loving and trusting life, we need to be willing to compare that with the areas where our life experiences aren't happy. We will find the exact opposite holds true.

If we will test every part of our lives, we will convince ourselves of the importance of having a positive concept of life. Then we can abandon our hate and fear, our separation and seclusion. We need to give ourselves the chance to see if it's true that life is safe by opening ourselves up, at least a little bit.

Active and Passive Forces

Now let's turn to the third member of this important triad: the healthy balance between being active and passive. Perhaps we've noticed in ourselves a strange and hard-to-explain distaste for being active and an equally odd hankering to be passive. This appears more strongly in some people than in others, but to whatever extent this shows up, it's necessary that we understand what's happening.

If we desire to be passive, this means we feel that being passive is better. It seems to promise a peacefulness that many confuse, unconsciously, with the state of being. The state of activity, then, is seen as a chore. It's a difficulty we fear we can't live up to and therefore would like to avoid. Why is this so?

First, we need to understand that this distorted idea comes from duality. The error lies in taking a fragment of unity and separating it from its complimentary fragment. In this way, activity is pitted as the opposite of passivity. In reality, in the highest states of consciousness, these two mingle so that the healthy state of activity is also, at the same time, passive, and vice versa. On the level of duality, this sounds like a contradiction.

We can demonstrate the truth of this point in our everyday life by seeing the way healthy activities are easy and effortless. Undertaking activity with a relaxed approach sounds passive, right? In this kind of healthy relaxation, we move without straining so our action has a peaceful rhythm. If we were to fragment off this rhythm of peace and experience it as a particle, it might seem like passivity.

Let's look at this concept from the other end. When we find ourselves dropping into a peaceful rhythm, we're never motionless. In this state of being—when we are in healthy passivity—the action of movement flows with the rhythm of the universe. It operates with the same unstrained motion of peace.

For a creative process to happen, there must always be a balance between the principles of activity and passivity. Said another way, without the harmony of these two forces complementing each another, the creative process is unthinkable. This applies to every single healthy activity on this planet, bar none. Even the balance between work and leisure are regulated by this principle.

Our work, when it arises from a healthy person, flows effortlessly, while our leisure can't be revitalizing if it's static and still. If we're totally still, of course, we are dead and that's not all that invigorating. Only life revives us, and life must move.

In the distortion of duality, we see activity as movement and passivity as standing still. Activity appears to ask us to exert strain, whereas passivity promises to relieve strain. In other words, we are back to seeing everything as basically good or bad. One side looks desirable, meaning the other must be undesirable.

Why do we see activity as the undesirable facet? Because it requires a sense of responsibility. It asks us to be grown up about dealing with the difficulties of life, so that the limitations of life gradually go away. So if we're totally identified with our ego, action then will seem frightening. For the ego is not designed to take action without being guided by the Real Self. It simply doesn't come preconfigured with the right properties for that.

So whenever we're not in touch with our Real Self, we're going to fear all the demands that being active makes on a person. And all the lip service in the world won't close the gap. Hence, being passive looks awfully tempting since, by its nature, it's not going to be demanding. Passivity comes without any fearsome obligations or expectations.

Then again, when we're exclusively identified with our egos and are neglecting the presence of our active side—which is a natural part of who we are—passivity is going to seem equally frightful. For in distortion, being passive is akin to being helpless. In a way, this makes sense. Because if we won't act purposefully—if we're rejecting and avoiding activity due to fear—we're not living in alignment with the universal laws inside us that always have our best interest at heart. As a result, we're at the mercy of circumstances outside ourselves, which are beyond our control.

Consequently, on one level we avoid activity, fearful we're not capable of carrying out whatever action is called for, while on another level we're afraid to stop and rest. When our ego can't tell the difference between healthy passivity and being stagnant, it tends to go into overdrive. We become overactive and more and more alienated from our Real Self.

So there's a one-to-one correlation between having a negative concept of life—which implies we're not in close contact with our innermost self—and being out of balance in our activity and passivity. The two things, in fact, are identical. If we're living in fear of our innermost self, why would we want to make contact with it? It would seem then that our only solution is to concentrate all our energy on our outer ego self. And this most assuredly disconnects us further from our Real Self and the life-giving powers that flow from within.

False Solutions

From here, we will go on to force ourselves to be in a loving state. Not only have we learned that this is what society expects from us, but also, we want to comply with our innermost conscience—our inner voice—that's never been completely snuffed out. Plus, we're hoping this is going to bring us the love, affection, approval, respect and acceptance we desire, without which we can't live.

Now we are forced to love from our ego-self, which is never going to work. The ego simply doesn't possess the power of love, so it can't give it. We're doomed to fail. If by chance, however, we do have some genuine love currents flowing from us, they have arisen from our innermost being. So whether we admit that such a place exists in us, they're coming into our personality through the back door, as it were.

If we've got that back door shut and locked tight, though, it will impossible for love to squeeze through. We'll be cut off from the stream of life and love, and that will show up in our feelings of emptiness and helplessness, despair and isolation. These of course don't feel good so we laboriously try to overcome them by loving from our ego. That's downright exhausting though, and the more exhausted we become, the more we shy away from activity which only seems like it will add strain to our already exhausted ego.

This looks like a good time to flee, and so off we go into the relief of passivity. As such, being passive seems incredibly desirable. But this kind of passivity is never fulfilling. It leaves us feeling more empty, increasingly dissatisfied, and more frightened. For that is the way of all false solutions. The farther we flee, the more apathetic we become, for naturally at this point, healthy passivity has slid all the way down into the distortion of apathy.

And so it is we find ourselves living in the pit of life with no invigorating life movement left. And this state, the lifeless state of apathy, is packed with a greater terror than any hurt or unhappiness.

Maybe now we can see that we really do need to contact our Real Self. We need to allow it to act, no matter how resistant or scared we feel. We might doubt it will work, but how about the alternative? The central idea here is to work on consolidating all our difficulties into one simple inner movement. Otherwise, without our Real Self, it won't be possible to find abundance and live in the wide-open expanses of life.

Getting Started

If we don't activate the Real Self, love can't come to us. This makes us feel isolated and distrustful, but our conscience isn't going to let us rest there. Even if much of our personality is open and loving, if there's a speck of non-lovingness left, our conscience isn't going to let that be. This may take any of a variety of forms, all of which will chip away at our ability to live our best life.

But when we are ready to establish contact with our true home base, our actions can be peaceful and our passivity can be enlivening. With the Real Self in charge, activity and passivity will walk in lockstep. Our reactions will be relaxed and meaningful and our actions will be desirable in themselves. Our passivity will hold no threat of being helpless. We'll be able to trust life and ourselves. All this is what rests on our deliberate activation of our innermost being.

Perhaps you hear an inner voice that says, "Oh yes, if only I could do that. Too bad I am not capable of wanting to contact my Real Self." If that's our attitude, we're likely waiting for a miracle to happen so we'll suddenly want to do the right thing. We're waiting as though something other than us will step in and inspire us to act. If that's the case, we might be waiting forever.

Consider the possibility that there's a nucleus of power and intelligence within that we need not fear. Think about giving it a chance. We can commit to this possibility, even if in this moment it's only a possibility. What do we have to lose? And how else might it come to life?

It won't arise based on theory or because something happens from the outside. We're the ones who must make it happen. If we make a start, even if it's tentative at first, our Real Self will gradually reveal itself and its reality to us. Our action is to commit to finding it.

Finding the Real Self

So just where is this life center we're committing to find? Is it located in our subtle bodies, or in our physical organs, or where? In truth, it's all of these places. For it is life itself, transcending everything and entering wherever there is an opening. By its very nature, it can't be more in one place and less in another. It's not a fixed spot.

That said, looking through our illusory lens of time, space and movement, the life center seems to be located down deep in our solar plexus, where we sense the pit of our stomach to be. This isn't completely an illusion, given that this actually is where we notice it the most. That's because this is where we are most receptive and open, and also most vulnerable.

When our Real Self is activated and not obstructed, it flows through every layer of our being. To the extent it is not activated, it can't reach the outer layers of our personality. When we are physically sick, our body remains inactive in the areas affected by the illness, and these correspond to the mental and emotional blocks—our distorted ideas and disharmonious feelings—that are involved.

When our outlook is sick—in other words, when we have a bad attitude— the Real Self is blocked off. So then its emanations can't penetrate into certain areas of our psyche. When that's the case, our Real Self does not show up in our outer personality but remains hidden in the depths of our soul. This is why our first task is to dismantle our Mask Self, penetrating past it so we can see the destructive attitudes we're hiding.

We're afraid to do this because we think our destructiveness is ultimately who we really are. We think our goodness only exists in our outer façade.

Only after we win this first battle can our destructive currents be properly released so they can reconvert to their original form. Then our hidden Real Self can begin to manifest.

This is the only way for the Real Self to come into our awareness and into reality. Once it's released—once we stop blocking it—it can surge through all the levels of our personality and heal our distortions. This is the way to become a totally self-realized person who is alive on all levels, physical as well as mental and emotional.

This activation and enlivened state is not going to come about overnight. Let's not forget how long we've been living with our fears, not only in this lifetime. We've conditioned ourselves to patterns of reacting that can't be broken up suddenly. This goes deeper than we know. These first inklings of awareness are a marvelous step and to get this far is already a tremendous victory on our spiritual path.

But we must come to realize how deeply entrenched fear is. We must become aware of all the specific reasons for our ingrained fears. We must want to understand what we already know on a deeper level. Then little by little, the heavy wall of fog will dissolve. All the mazes of confusion that cover up the Real Self, with its wonderful, strong feelings, will become clear. Our preliminary insights will continue to unfold when we observe our reactions and utter the wish to feel love in our whole person, including our physical body.

Evolving

To love is to live. It is to have an attitude of openness and inclusion, and to move towards another. When such movement is lacking, that is not love. That is not living, and so that is death. When we fear that life is dangerous and hostile, we defend ourselves against it. This is an error in our understanding of life, and duality is the result of erroneous concepts. Death, then, including physical death, is precisely the result of duality.

If we are here, living in duality, we must be in error somewhere. And error equates to nonlove, which is directly opposed to life as it really is. And how is life really? It is potential, waiting and ready to unfold whenever it is allowed to, wherever truthful, appropriate concepts stand so that nothing is blocking its way. This life that we are living is a continuum that flows in a constantly moving process. We are able to sense this only when our personal psyche is following its own life-movement. This formula is as reliable as any mathematical equation.

So then if we reach our Real Self and are able to love, we'll never die, right? In truth, it's all a matter of degree. Inorganic life is the closest thing we know of to the state of life where there is no love. Total love, on the other end of the spectrum, is when we have no more inner splits due to false concepts. That's when universal consciousness—unity, oneness—can be completely realized. Then there will be no more duality, so no more life and death. To get there, we each have to walk very slowly through all the many stages of evolution. Right now, we are working our way through this interim stage of being human.

Let's say we realize, after reading these teachings or by doing our personal work, that we've never really loved anything or anyone. Now we want to find our Real Self. The place to start is by asking ourselves to what extent we believe life is against us, causing us to not love. We need to write down our specific ideas: In what particular respect do I assume life is against me?

If our answer is, "In all ways," we haven't gone far enough. It doesn't suffice to make general admissions, for that's not quite accurate. We have to be specific. Then, when our list is complete, we can begin to wonder: "Maybe it's not this way after all." We have to make allowances for the possibility that maybe, just maybe, we are mistaken.

Often we create a bottleneck in our progress on our path by not moving away from a wrong conclusion. We have found a hidden wrong belief, we know in principle it's wrong—it must be wrong if it creates disharmony—but we double down, saying, "Yes, but this is how I feel." Then we sit and wait to feel differently without making any effort on our part.

The way to solve our problems is by seriously questioning our conclusions and admitting that maybe things could be different. We must make room for the truth. And truth can't enter into a closed, dark room filled with misconceptions about life and about the nature of who we truly are at our core.

Universal Connectivity

When we are at one with the center of our being, we will be united with the universal core of everyone else. From there we can reach out with love and touch others, whether they are currently in a human body or not. Everything will fall into place and unify.

This is how we can reach loved ones who have passed on. Not by being in touch with a specific individual in the nonphysical world, but by connecting with all beings, wherever they are. For to attempt to establish individual contact with someone who has died is not really helpful for anyone concerned. It shifts the emphasis away from what really is important—clearing away what is blocking us from contact with our own innermost self—to something that is not really important.

In the end, it is far more truthful and more loving to put our emphasis on what really matters: self-realization. Then love with other incarnated people will happen in the best possible way. By contrast, making contact with people who are no longer in their bodies can never be as fulfilling, ever. It must lead, in some way, to an escape from what is most important to emphasize.

People who seek the comfort of contacting a deceased loved one do so to alleviate their doubt and their pain. But it never really accomplishes that in a genuine, lasting way. Only by doing our personal work of self-development can we find lasting peace. But if we're not willing to do this work and unwind our erroneous concepts, no one else can help us.

The moment we want to move beyond our current limitations, however, help will reach us from all sides. Then we'll be able to receive the love, strength and truth that's in the air all around us. Our gaze will adjust and our perceptions will change, to the degree that love, strength and truth are activated in our core and we're uniting with others.

"Be in peace. Be in truth. Be in yourself!"
–The Pathwork Guide

Chapter 9

Our Fundamental Fear of Bliss

Every person on Earth has an apparently nonsensical fear of bliss to some extent. Even though it makes no sense, there it is, and this fear exists side-by-side with our longing for bliss. Yet bliss is our birthright. We have every right to live in a state of supreme bliss and sublime joy, which are qualities we struggle to adequately describe in any language.

No matter how unhappy we are, somewhere deep inside we haven't forgotten that this fear is not natural. Indeed, if this weren't the case, it would be far easier to accept our frustrations in life. For what does it mean to be unhappy if not to be frustrated about not having what we want? Embedded in our unhappiness, then, is the promise that the opposite could be true: we could be happy. Since both are present, we feel ambivalent about how we should be experiencing life. From this follows another ambivalence: Is it OK to long for pleasure, or should we fear it?

For some of us, we have much less fear than desire. If this is us, we feel relatively fulfilled and our lives are rich and joyful. We have a deep capacity to experience pleasure, and we have a trusting attitude toward life. Since our concept of life is positive, life expands. For us, it's not that hard to overcome our remaining defenses and fears that close off expanding further into bliss.

Most people, however, fear happiness more than they desire it. If this is us, we will basically be unhappy, feeling life is passing us by. Life will seem meaningless and like we somehow missed out on it. Our capacity for experiencing pleasure will be very limited. We will be numb and mired in apathy. In our lifeless state we won't trust and will be withdrawn from life, and we will resist looking within ourselves for the cause of our suffering.

When we have a heavy fear-to-desire ratio, our negative concept of life seems to justify our defenses, and we fear expanding into a different state of consciousness. Our fears cause us to hang on desperately to the very state that's responsible for our plight in life. This is the sorry predicament so many of us find ourselves in.

There is another subset of people who have an even balance between fear and desire for happiness. If this is us, we have areas of our lives that are abundant, successful and fulfilling. But we also have areas where we experience the opposite. The more we poke around in our psyche, the more apparent it becomes that where we are happy, fearless and free, we feel fulfilled. And where we are afraid of the best life can offer, we are not fulfilled. This is a mathematical equation that always comes out right in the end.

Awareness

Of course, we're usually unaware that we fear what we want the most. Plus, the further away the thing we want is, the easier it is to overlook our fear of it. But as it comes closer, and as we sincerely question our reactions, we'll find that on the inside, we're closing the doors. Our shrinking away may be so subtle it's easy to miss. But this is exactly what we need to bring out into the open.

This part may not be easy to find. For some, especially those who aren't yet acquainted with the nature of the human unconscious, this concept— that we fear what we most long for—may be hard to swallow. And yet it's true: The thing we cry the most for is the thing we fear the most. But if we will notice the places where taking the tiniest risk seems like too much, then we have a clue. For we tend to cringe from what we want, preferring to play it safe and stick with a gray life.

Once we've found this tendency in ourselves, we're starting to make progress toward freedom. Now we're catching on that our own hidden thoughts, emotions and attitudes are what create our fate. That, and nothing else. This discovery has the potential to rock our world. Before then, our tension and suffering will be all that much greater, because we won't understand what's causing them.

When we feel like we're the victim of a hazardous world, and we think we have to defend ourselves, we drift farther and farther from the center of truth. The more self-alienated we become, the more we blame the world for causing our alienation, which brings us less and less relief. No matter how wrong the other may be, making them merit our blame, this never removes our suffering. No matter how much we can bend others to comply with our wishes, this never moves the meter on our feelings of emptiness.

And we will go on suffering as long we remain unaware that the blocks closing us off from what we want the most are in us. For that long, we will feel like life is futile. We'll feel helpless and nothing we do will lessen our pain of feeling unfulfilled. There we will teeter between bitterness and self-pity, between distorted self-blame and projecting all our misfortunes onto life and others. In no way will we sense we deserve the best life has to offer.

Our Inner No

So what's the first step we can take to release the lever on this block? We must truly know and experience our own rejection of pleasure. At first, we are apt to fight this truth, tooth and nail. For many of us, we'd rather stay dependent on outer circumstances, even though accepting the great truth that we hold the key to freedom in our hands is the most joyful discovery we'll ever make on this path.

Once we see the full impact of this truth, we'll see that there is indeed only one way out. But we'll never see the beauty of this reality if we're still battling against it. True independence, then, will continue to elude us.

Often, when we sense that there could be more to life than we are now experiencing, we become cynical, and we resign ourselves to what we have. But those who are courageously walking a spiritual path of self-discovery have decided to take a different tack: We are willing to search for where we say No. We come to understand that the more strained and compulsive we feel, and the more urgent and impatient our striving for fulfillment is, the more certain we can be that underneath is just as rigid a No as on the surface there is an urgent Yes.

The surface urge is really not helping anything. In fact, it's as big a hindrance as our underground No, because our surface Yes is made out of fear and distortion. Our urgent Yes is born of the unconscious knowledge that inside we're blocking off a Yes. Now this doesn't mean that if there's no urgent Yes toward fulfillment on the surface, there's not a hidden No below. Some people just behave differently than others. Or it could just mean we've given up. Whatever the situation, we won't be able to relax a painful, anxious urge until we find personally and specifically how we say No to what we want the most.

Standing in Truth

Through all of these teachings from the Pathwork Guide, we are being taught about the human condition. For instance, when we ignore how we deny our own fulfillment, we are creating difficulties for ourselves. When we project what we lack as being outside of ourselves—placing blame on circumstances or other people—we create more frictions and constrictions for ourselves. We create confusion and more entanglements, ultimately becoming more dependent.

If we continue to look away from our inner obstructions, preferring to believe that others or fate are the cause of all our problems, we then can't help but live in tension and fear. So we can see that awareness—of our own obstructions—determines everything. With this understanding, we can comprehend the true meaning of self-responsibility.

Now let's connect these ideas with a deeper understanding of this all-important mystery: Why do we say No to our deepest desire for the most intense bliss imaginable? What makes happiness seem dangerous and therefore undesirable? Let's focus our light in this direction.

To whatever degree we reject ourselves, to that degree we will not be able to bear happiness or sustain pleasure. And why do we reject ourselves? In fact, all self-rejection falls into one of two camps.

First, there is a kind of self-rejection that's based on a precision instrument inside us, if you will, that can measure where and in exactly what way we have broken spiritual laws. It knows where we have attempted to cheat life, hoping to get more than we wish to give. It knows all about our little hidden games of deception, and it sees how we dramatize and pretend we are better than we are, not daring to be who and how we actually are, right now.

When we do this, we don't really love, we just pretend to love, hoping to get something in return. But the key to the universe is real love, not fake love, like the clinging, bartering love we often give. Genuine love lives and lets others live in freedom; it can take No for an answer. False love works more like a lasso that wants to dominate and hold tight. It may seem like we can fool others with our false love, but our real inner self cannot be deceived.

Where do we come up short in terms of generosity? Do we have a different yardstick for how others should measure up versus ourselves? All these violations go on all the time, and our Real Self is keeping notes. Meanwhile, our conscious mind is busy blotting out the truth, and in this way, we commit the gravest violation of them all. It's one thing that we do these things, but it's worse that we inwardly lie to cover them up.

Our pretenses deny and falsify the record, creating a double violation. And this leads to the most painful state, mentally and emotionally. We become caught in this double bind from which there appears to be no exit. Until, that is, we start to see what we've been doing. We must uncover our violations, own up to our inner lies, and let it all go.

What does that look like, this housecleaning we all need to do? Let's say we are selfish. If we pretend like our selfishness is really just us being self-assertive, we're rationalizing, and that creates a layer of falsehood. Or maybe we have a cruel streak, or we hate. If we only feel cruelty and hate in secret, and only act it out indirectly so that it looks like its opposite, we can add hypocrisy to our list of crimes against humanity.

Our hypocrisy may be out in the open for all to see, or we might hide it extremely well. It's just as poisonous either way. But if, on the other hand, we have the courage to admit what we're up to, and can look at ourselves squarely and honestly, we will have already made great strides in overcoming our violation.

By accepting the truth about ourselves, we step into a general climate of truth. Now we're standing on a platform from which we just might be able to work ourselves out of our harmful behaviors. For sure, we'll still struggle with it. But now we can start to understand it. By meditating for help and guidance, our feelings may spontaneously change.

For we may have a change of heart now that we are operating in alignment with spiritual laws. In addition, by accepting our present state, we are setting up inner conditions that are compatible with bliss. Maybe we have to admit, "I can't help feeling this way, even though I don't like it and I know it's destructive." At least now we are being truthful, and we are making room for change.

Anything in us that goes against the grain of truth and love makes our being unable to sustain happiness, for happiness is a powerful positive energy. It takes more strength to be happy than to be unhappy, and we acquire this strength by facing the truth and shedding our illusions about life.

Perfectionism

The second reason we reject ourselves is because of our imaginary violations when we don't live up to our unrealistic standards of perfection. Perfectionism, as we all know, has extremely demanding and rigid ideals. Our efforts to adhere to them stem from yet another violation of spiritual law, and not because we are overdosing on morality.

Perfectionism sprouts from our pride and vanity, our need to be in control, our pretense, and our fear of standing up for ourselves. In short, it amounts to being untrue to ourselves out of greed for approval and admiration. So whenever we can't accept our own humanity, including our current limitations, we are violating universal law. Then the climate of our psyche is not compatible with that bliss we all long for.

Sound simple? It's really not. For when we embark on a path of inner exploration, self-rejection can be hard to find, and the reasons behind it even more obscure. Typically, we're only aware of what we're pretending *to ourselves* to be. For example, if we've locked certain emotions away because we can't bear feeling them, we genuinely believe they are gone. Then we kid ourselves that we already know all about ourselves.

Therefore, it's not that easy to find out how we're really operating. We'll need to point ourselves in a new direction to develop a new awareness of the emotional reactions we've habitually been glossing over. But our awareness of how we violate spiritual law will reveal, in equal measure, an awareness of how we are rejecting happiness.

Whether we're just starting out on a spiritual path, haven't yet begun, or have been making some pretty good headway, the advice is the same: Find the place in life where something seems to be missing, where you want to have more feelings or experience more intensely, and go in that direction. Find what you don't accept in yourself. Close your eyes and see what you don't like. Search for the obscure but tangible reaction that pushes away pleasure. Become willing to see what you haven't seen before.

With this approach, we will experience, one step at a time, where we push a part of ourselves away. Over time, as we stop doing that, we'll become better equipped to have happy feelings. It takes a fine awareness to pick up subtle soul movements that pull back when something good comes along. When we discover this, the rage that blames others, life or circumstances will subside.

With this, the poisonous clouds floating through our psyche will lift, making our inner home compatible with the bliss we have every right to enjoy. Accepting the truth in ourselves, then, is synonymous with accepting happiness. We can't have one without the other.

There's a third leg on this inner stool, and it's recognizing the creative substance that's molding our lives. For nothing that happens is haphazard. There's no outside power deciding how much fulfillment we get to have. There's no force sending us pain or suffering. There's no frustration we're required to bear. In fact, unfulfillment isn't so much self-punishment as it is inner pollution that squelches bliss and joy. We ignore the truth of what we are and do, and don't realize that this is what creates hazards. The only way to clear such obstructions is self-responsibility. We need to face ourselves head on.

Asking for Help

Truth is what creates inner security, trust and fearlessness; ignorance is what creates fear. And fear causes us to close up. Then our mind won't use the powerful creative substance—the stuff we use to mold our lives—to create expansion, and we will instead invest in tightening up our perimeter with defenses.

Just as stagnation and frustration belong together, expansion and bliss are a matched set. This means we can't expand—we can't bring all our potential out into the world—unless we're in a state of joyousness. Simply put, bliss is necessary for expansion.

The process of expansion is self-activating, and it blends the masculine and feminine principles—also referred to as activity and passivity—in perfect harmony. But if we fear expansion—in other words, we fear bliss—we'll also fear growing and changing. So we do, in fact, fear our own built-in powers to create.

Like happiness, the qualities of pleasure, bliss and fulfillment require a lot of inner firmness and strength. Remember, being unhappy takes less strength than being happy. How do we generate this strength? By intentionally calling on the divine powers within ourselves. In response, they will help us sustain bliss, guiding us to not inadvertently close up against happiness.

Such prayers for support shouldn't be saved for when our lives are in crisis. For when we're happy we're in a good place for becoming even more compatible with the creative powers that will make us better equipped for sustaining bliss. Then when we're unhappy, it's important we look at it as a meaningful lesson that can help lead us to further growth. Doing this will require contact with the innate wisdom that resides with these superior forces. So any day of the week is a good day to be asking for help and guidance.

Maybe we're already accessing all the help, strength and inspiration we can receive through meditation. Perhaps we already know how effective divine contact is, how unfailing its response, and how unimaginable its wisdom. Yet during times of upheaval, when we're involved in deep conflicts, we simply "forget." But there will come a point when it won't be so hard to remember to make contact, and we'll become more proficient at using it when times are tough. This is indeed a key, to enlist these powers all the time.

The Energy Centers

Many of us are aware that all humans have certain energy centers, or chakras, within our beings. Each of these energy centers is related to a mental attitude. So when we change from being ignorant, fearful, self-alienated, hostile and distrusting, to becoming open, truthful, trustful and loving, our energy centers will open up.

Since there is an intimate connection between our spirit, mind and body, such an opening up—or waking up—will result in a distinct experience in the body. This is why our approach on this path of self-realization must include the whole personality.

As we learn to ascertain when a center is open, we'll be able to use its energy to find the mental attitude associated with it. Likewise, we will see there's a connection between our fear of pleasure and our energy centers. For when we're in fear, these centers must necessarily be closed and cramped. As such, the life force can't get in.

But when we open ourselves up to joy, pleasure and happiness on all levels of our being, our relaxed attitude of "letting be" will eventually open up these centers. Our work of developing self-awareness, facing the truth, and creating an inner connection with the universal forces of life, then, will enliven our entire being by activating these centers.

Most people walk around in a perpetually cramped state with clenched energy centers. Yet we've all incarnated precisely to discover the truth of spiritual laws and to see how we are out of alignment with them. When we stop deceiving ourselves, we will relax deeply, and in this undefended state our whole personality will come alive and be sweetly attuned with life.

The Universal Self

We can liken a functioning personality to an overall center, like a planet. Then imagine there is another center that is timeless and spaceless. This is the center of absolutely everything that ever has lived, is living, and will live. This universal center is so huge, it's the same for everyone and everything.

Fully self-realized personality planets are always in the orbit of this universal spiritual center. They are open to it and therefore totally exposed to it. They're never out of its sight and are always influenced by it. Their movements are completely in sync with it.

But most personality planets are more or less off-center. We have somehow managed to move out of the field of vision of the universal center, such that we are not exposed to it. Although the universal center never wavers, we sometimes close our personalities off to it, moving out of its field of vision, as it were.

At times we step wholly into the universal field; at other times we move out. Being in or out of tune with the universal source determines our level of aliveness and alignment with the truth.

When positive attitudes carry the day—including self-awareness and self-acceptance—we are tuning into love and trust. In short, we are becoming more like the universal life center. We are converging. Our personality center will become charged and enlivened by the universal one, until we are soaked up by it.

When this happens, our personality will not be annihilated. The self will not be destroyed. For all of life actually already exists in the spiritual center, which enlivens everything. Death simply means we have become separated from the center, such that its light can't shine on our personality and infuse it with energy.

Never lose sight of the fact that life is intrinsically safe. This is an unchangeable fact that no amount of separation from the spiritual center can deny. Ultimately, as long as we keep going, we'll come to see the truth of this greater reality, and we'll reunite with all that is.

"Be God!"
–The Pathwork Guide

Ways to learn more

2 Fully facing our fear of loving

- *LIVING LIGHT,* Chapter 2: Mobility in relaxation
- *LIVING LIGHT,* Chapter 10: The five stages of love
- *BIBLE ME THIS*: Releasing the riddles of Holy Scripture
- *BONES*, Chapter 14: Exposing the mistaken image we have about God

3 Finding freedom and peace by overcoming fear of the unknown

- *THE PULL*, Chapter 1: The cosmic pull toward union
- *THE PULL*, Chapter 11: Man and woman
- *THE PULL*, Chapter 12: Self-fulfillment through self-realization as a man or a woman
- *GEMS*, Chapter 11: Four avenues for reaching the cosmic nougat at our core

4 Finding true abundance by going through our fear

- *SPIRITUAL LAWS*: Hard & fast logic for forging ahead

5 Giving up our fear-filled struggle to guard our secrets

- *FINDING GOLD*, Chapter 5: Self-alienation and the way back to the Real Self
- *BONES*, Chapter 7: Love, power and serenity in divinity or in distortion

7 How fear of releasing the little ego spoils happiness

- *BONES*, Chapter 16: How pleasure gets twisted into self-perpetuating cycles of pain
- *GEMS*, Chapter 7: Rolling with change and overcoming fear of death

8 Three things that underpin self-fulfillment

- *BONES*, Chapter 12: Finding out the truth about ourselves, including our faults
- *SPILLING THE SCRIPT,* Masks & Defenses

9 Our fundamental fear of bliss

- *BONES*, Chapter 15: Learning to speak the language of the unconscious
- *PEARLS*, Chapter 9: Why flubbing on perfection is the way to find joy

What is Pathwork®?

This remarkable collection of spiritual teachings about facing our fears has been selected by Jill Loree from the body of material collectively known as the Pathwork spiritual materials. The teachings of the Pathwork are contained in about 250 lectures that were given in the 1950s, '60s and '70s by a Vienna-born New Yorker named Eva Pierrakos. The teachings are unparalleled in their wisdom, scope and practicality, and therefore also in their effectiveness.

By following these Pathwork teachings, we embark on a lifelong spiritual journey of self-discovery that allows us to heal our emotional wounds, understand the true workings of life, and foster harmony and balance within our own being, as well as with others and God.

Perhaps the least interesting thing to know about these lectures is that they were channeled. This relevant-yet-insignificant fact is often one of the first things that tumbles out when one tries to explain the Pathwork. It is a relevant point of interest because this material is often of great interest to people who have curious minds and would like to understand the origin of these teachings. At the same time, it is insignificant because it doesn't really matter where they came from. As the Guide often said, you shouldn't believe anything—no matter who said it—unless it makes sense to you.

Who is the Pathwork Guide?

The Guide is the entity who is actually speaking, using Eva as the medium, or channel, through which he spoke. Owed to Eva's dedication to her task—including her willingness to do her own work—the material continually evolved and deepened over the course of the 22 years she gave monthly lectures.

Pathwork is a trademarked word owned by the Pathwork Foundation, a non-profit organization. It was coined along the way by Eva and other followers of the Guide based on the fact that he so often spoke of "being on a path," and the reality that it is hard work to follow such a path.

In truth, every human being is on a spiritual path, whether they know it or not. Today, however, many more people are becoming conscious about their spiritual journey. For hard as it may be to look directly at our own faults and negativity, at some point we realize we can't keep looking away from ourselves and hope to find solutions. And that, in a way, is the heart of what the Guide teaches: The only way to get to the other side of our struggles in life is by stepping through the gateway of self-responsibility.

The lectures are all now available online in the form of printed transcripts, free audio recordings and, for a fee, the original recordings by Eva:

www.pathwork.org

What is Phoenesse®?

The Guide offers profound teachings that are only valuable if they are put into service in understanding and unwinding our everyday disharmonies, both large and small. One has to actively apply the Guide's teachings to be served by them. That's really the key.

But the lectures are long—roughly 10-12 pages each—and dense, so it takes some mental stamina to get through them. This is where Phoenesse can help.

Doing the Work

Inspired directly by the Guide, Phoenesse offers a fresh approach to these timeless spiritual teachings. Phoenesse—pronounced "finesse"—is a registered service mark of Phoenesse LLC, founded by Jill Loree.

In the *Real. Clear.* spiritual book series, Jill Loree has rewritten nearly 100 of the teachings using easier-to-read language, and organized them by topic. Podcasts of each teaching are also available online.

In the *Self.Care.* teaching series, Jill Loree offers a high-level overview of the work, identifying the various parts of the self and showing how to actually go about doing the work of healing.

You can also read an overview of the Guide's teachings on the Phoenesse website:

www.phoenesse.com

What is The Guide Speaks?

After each lecture, attendees were encouraged to ask questions. In addition, once a month Eva and the Guide would hold dedicated Question & Answer sessions. Unlike the original lectures, which were prepared by a council of spiritual beings, the Guide answered these questions himself. For this reason, the Q&As embody a somewhat different energy from the lectures, which—in addition to their shorter length—makes them easier to digest.

The Q&As were either related to the lecture just given, to a person's personal issues, or to life in general. They offer a wisdom and perspective that has the potential to change a person's worldview. Jill Loree has sorted the thousands of questions into topics to make the answers more accessible, and has made them available for free online:

www.theguidespeaks.com

Find answers to questions related to the topic of fear:

Fear | General

Fear & Hostility in Relationship

Fear of Abandonment

Fear of Another

Fear of Being Destroyed

Fear of Being in the Now

Fear of Change

Fear of Closeness

Fear of Commitment

Fear of Criticism

Fear of Death
Fear of Good Feelings
Fear of Letting Go
Fear of Losing Good Feelings
Fear of Love
Fear of Making Decisions
Fear of Murder
Fear of Opening Up
Fear of People
Fear of Public Speaking
Fear of Rejection
Fear of Self
Fear of Sex
Fear of Success
Fear of Surpassing Parents
Fear of The Unknown
Overcoming Fear
Phobias

About the Author

Jill Loree | Founder of Phoenesse

Jill Loree
Founder of Phoenesse

A neatnik with a ready sense of humor, Jill Loree's first job as a root-beer-stand carhop in northern Wisconsin was an early sign that things could only get better.

She would go on to throw pizzas and bartend while in college, before discovering that the sweet spot of her 30-year sales-and-marketing career would be in business-to-business advertising. A true Gemini, she has a degree in chemistry and a flair for writing. Her brain fires on both the left and right sides.

That said, her real passion in life has been her spiritual path. Raised in the Lutheran faith, she became a more deeply spiritual person in the rooms of Alcoholics Anonymous, a spiritual recovery program, starting in 1989. In 1997, she was introduced to the wisdom of the Pathwork, which she describes as "having walked through the doorway of a fourth step and found the whole library."

She completed four years of Pathwork Helpership training in 2007 followed by four years of apprenticing and discernment before stepping into her full Helpership in 2011. She has been a teacher in the Transformation

Program offered at Sevenoaks Retreat Center in Madison, Virginia, operated by Mid-Atlantic Pathwork, where she also led marketing activities for over two years and served on the Board of Trustees.

In 2012, Jill completed four years of kabbalah training in a course called the Soul's Journey, achieving certification for hands-on healing using the energies embodied in the tree of life.

Not bad for a former pom-pom squad captain who once played Dolly in *Hello Dolly!* She is now the proud mom of two adult children, Charlie and Jackson, who were born and raised in Atlanta. Jill Loree is delighted to be married to Scott Wisler, but continues to use her middle name as her last (it's pronounced loh-REE). In her spare time she enjoys reading, writing, yoga, golf, skiing and hiking, especially in the mountains.

In 2014, she consciously decoupled from the corporate world and is now dedicating her life to writing and teaching about spirituality, personal healing and self-discovery.

Catch up with Jill at www.phoenesse.com.

phoene&e
FIND YOUR TRUE YOU.

More from Phoenesse

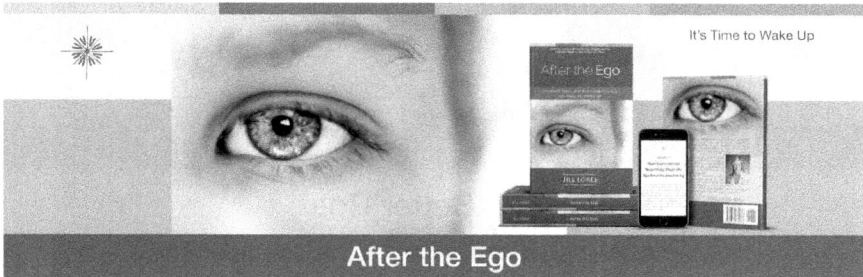

After the Ego

After the Ego
Insights from the Pathwork® Guide on How to Wake Up

Whether or not we lead meaningful and fulfilling lives depends entirely on the relationship between our ego and our Real Self. All these teachings from the Pathwork Guide are pointing to this, prying at it from a multitude of directions to help us open to this truth as our personal experience. For if this relationship is in balance, everything falls nicely into place.

But now, as a new world unfolds from the new consciousness sweeping Earth, many are struggling to find their footing. What every soul on Earth is actually noticing is where they currently stand on their personal journey to find their Real Self and live from this truthful inner space.

After the Ego reveals key facets of the complex and fascinating phenomenon behind the inner "earthquakes" now shaking so many people, and walks us through the vital process of awakening from duality.

Now is the moment for all of us to pay attention—not just to the unprecedented outer events in our world, but to what is happening within.

Now is the time to wake up.

Spiritual Essays — phoenesse — Get a **Better Boat**

Get a Better Boat
Trustworthy Teachings for Difficult Times

If we build our house on sand, it might last for a while. But eventually things will start to crumble and collapse. We may even have forgotten we decided long ago to build on sand. That doesn't change the reality of the situation though.

Over time, anything not built on a solid foundation of truth is bound to eventually collapse. It must. So it can be rebuilt the right way.

The era that's now arriving is going to further shake whatever is not sound, whatever has been built on sand. We must collectively come to realize that the only way to get to the other side of our challenges is by waking up and stepping through the doorway of self-responsibility. And that's exactly what the Pathwork Guide is showing us how to do in this collection of 33 spiritual essays.

Jill Loree began working deeply with the Pathwork teachings in 1997. In 2014, she began working full time to make them easier to access. Now, in *Get a Better Boat*, she crafts a clear message—a beacon of light—to help us navigate these difficult times.

The spiritual teachings in this book are now 50 years old. Yet these timeless teachings are proven and deeply trustworthy. They chart a highly spiritual—and very practical—way to journey through the seas of life. If you let them, they can become your better boat.

Learn About **Self-Transformation**

Understand these Spiritual Teachings

Read an overview of the Pathwork Guide's teachings about personal self-development on the Phoenesse website. This profound spiritual wisdom is presented in three parts:

- **The Work of Healing:** Learn about the work of incarnating as a human into this land of duality, and the steps we can take to unwind our difficulties and free ourselves from struggle.
- **The Prequel:** Learn about the series of events that unfolded in the Spirit World, landing us here in this difficult dimension.
- **The Rescue:** Learn what happened when we lost our free will, how we got it back, and who we should thank.

www.phoenesse.com

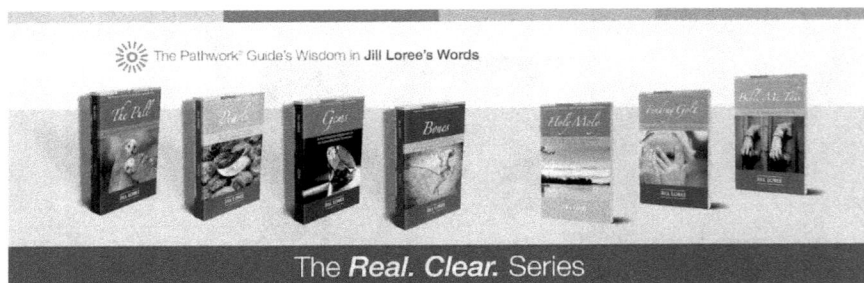

The Pathwork® Guide's Wisdom in **Jill Loree's Words**

The *Real. Clear.* Series

Real. Clear.
A Seven-Book Series of Spiritual Teachings

The *Real. Clear.* series offers a fresh approach to timeless spiritual teachings by way of easier-to-read language; it's the Pathwork Guide's wisdom in Jill Loree's words. Each book is written with a bit of levity because, as Mary Poppins put it, "A spoonful of sugar helps the medicine go down."

HOLY MOLY: The Story of Duality, Darkness and a Daring Rescue

There's one story, as ancient and ageless as anything one can imagine, that lays a foundation on which all other truths stand. It exposes the origin of opposites. It illuminates the reality of darkness in our midst. It speaks of herculean efforts made on our behalf. This is that story.

FINDING GOLD: The Search for Our Own Precious Self

The journey to finding the whole amazing nugget of the Real Self is a lot like prospecting for gold. Both combine the lure of potential and the excitement of seeing a sparkling possibility, with needing to have the patience of a saint.

It helps to have a map of our inner landscape and a headlamp for seeing into dark corners. That's what Jill Loree has created in this collection of spiritual teachings called *Finding Gold.*

BIBLE ME THIS: Releasing the Riddles of Holy Scripture

The Bible is a stumper for many of us, not unlike the Riddler teasing Batman with his "riddle me this" taunts. But what if we could know what some of those obscure passages mean? What's the truth hidden in the myth of Adam & Eve? And what was up with that Tower of Babel?

Bible Me This is a collection of in-depth answers to a variety of questions asked of the Guide about the Bible.

THE PULL: Relationships & Their Spiritual Significance

The Pull is about discovering the truth about relationships: they are the doorway through which we ultimately can come to know ourselves, God and another person; through them, we can learn to fully live. Because while life may be many things, more than anything else, it is all about relationships.

The Pull walks us through the delicate dance of intimate relationships, helping us navigate one of the most challenging aspects of life.

PEARLS: A Mind-Opening Collection of 17 Fresh Spiritual Teachings

In this classic, practical collection, Jill Loree strings together timeless spiritual teachings, each carefully polished with a light touch. Topics include: Privacy & Secrecy • The Lord's Prayer • Political Systems • The Superstition of Pessimism • Preparing to Reincarnate • Our Relationship to Time • Grace & Deficit • The Power of Words • Perfectionism • Authority • Order • Positive Thinking • Three Faces of Evil • Meditation for Three Voices • The Spiritual Meaning of Crisis • Leadership • Letting Go & Letting God

GEMS: A Multifaceted Collection of 16 Clear Spiritual Teachings

Clear and radiant, colorful and deep, each sparkling gem in this collection of spiritual teachings taken mostly from the final 50 lectures out of nearly 250, offers a ray of light to help illuminate our steps to reaching oneness.

BONES: A Building-Block Collection of 19 Fundamental Spiritual Teachings

This collection is like the bones of a body—a framework around which the remaining body of work can arrange itself. Sure, there's a lot that needs to be filled in to make it all come to life, but with *Bones*, now we've got the basic building blocks in place.

NUTSHELLS: Short & Sweet Spiritual Insights

Nutshells are short-and-sweet daily spiritual insights carved from three books: *Pearls*, *Gems* and *Bones*. Meaningful inspirations and memorable phrases are woven together to create a new creation that largely resembles the original form. Like the acorn that contains the potential for the oak tree, these nuggets of wisdom hold the power to change our whole perspective on life.

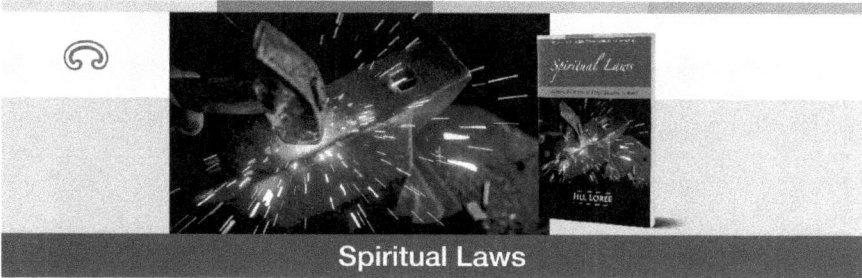

Spiritual Laws

Spiritual Laws
Hard & Fast Logic for Forging Ahead

Just what are the laws that rule this precious land? Turns out, there are an infinite number of laws that govern everything that happens. And while *Spiritual Laws* does not claim to be comprehensive in covering them all, this sampling of teachings from the Pathwork Guide does a nice job of explaining how this sphere works.

Understanding this will help us grasp the truth that behind our trials, there is a method. That someone or something is behind life, working out a plan. So gather round and listen up, because there are important guidelines we could all stand to know more about, and the hammer is about to drop.

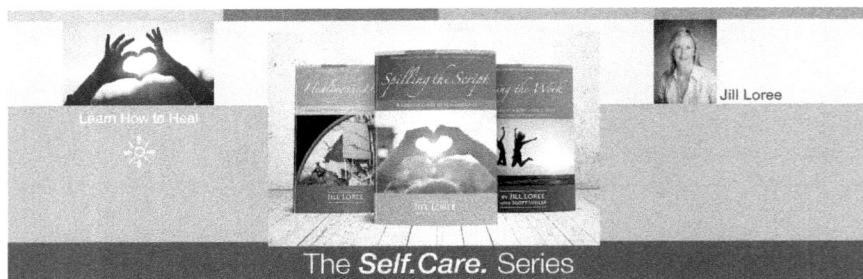

The *Self.Care.* Series

Self. Care.
A Three-Book Teaching Series

The *Self. Care.* How-to-Heal series offers a bird's-eye view of the Pathwork Guide's teachings and shows us how to apply them in working with ourselves and others.

SPILLING THE SCRIPT: A Concise Guide to Self-Knowing

Now, for the first time, powerful spiritual teachings from the Guide are available in one concise book. Jill Loree has written *Spilling the Script* to deliver a clear, high-level perspective about self-discovery and healing, giving us the map we need for following this life-changing path to oneness.

The goal of this spiritual journey is to make contact with our divine core so we can transition from living in duality to discovering the joy of being in unity. For even as we believe ourselves to be victims of an unfair universe, the truth is that we are continually guarding ourselves against pain, and through our defended approach to life we unknowingly bring about our current life circumstances. But we can make new choices.

Bit by bit, as we come out of the trance we have been in, we begin to see cause and effect, and to take responsibility for the state of our lives. Gradually, our lives transform. We once again can sense our essential nature and eternal connectedness with all that is.

"You will find how you cause all your difficulties. You have already stopped regarding these words as mere theory, but the better you progress, the more will you truly understand just how and why you cause your hardships. By so doing, you gain the key to changing your life."
–Pathwork Guide, Lecture #78

HEALING THE HURT: How to Heal Using Spiritual Guidance

The work of healing our fractured inner selves takes a little finesse, a lot of stick-to-it-iveness, and the skilled help of someone who has gone down this road before. Being a Helper then is about applying all we have learned on our own healing journey to help guide others through the process of re-unifying their fragmented hidden places.

That may sound simple, but it's surely not easy. It's also not easy to be the Worker, the one who does this work of spiritual healing. Now, with *Healing the Hurt*, everyone can understand the important skills needed by a Helper to assure Workers find what they're looking for.

DOING THE WORK: Healing Our Body, Mind & Spirit by Getting to Know the Self | By Jill Loree with Scott Wisler

Many of us have an inkling there can be more to life: that more meaningful moments are possible, and more satisfying experiences are attainable. Well, we're right. And fortunately, the tools for bringing this about are not really a secret. They're just not obvious. Herein lies the crux of the problem. We must come to realize what we have not been willing or able to see before.

Truth be told, no one gets out of planet Earth alive. But we can come out ahead by learning to make the best use of our time here. And that starts the day we begin doing the work. So let's get at it.

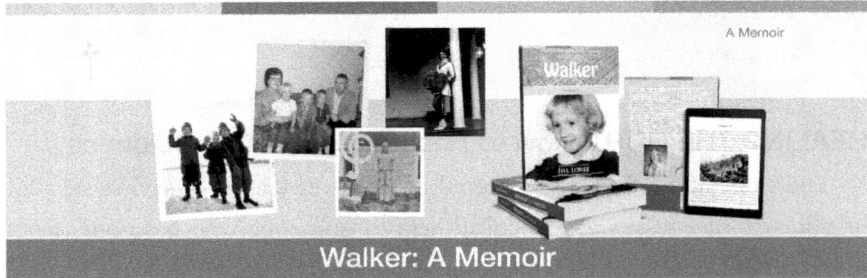

Walker: A Memoir

Walker
A Memoir

Walker is a memoir about one woman's spiritual journey to open her heart and develop compassion. Through it all, her own gumption would be her steady companion.

It starts out with a young girl raised in a singing Lutheran family where things looked good on the outside. But inside, Jill Loree was struggling. Later, she would "trudge the dreary road of happy destiny," as the AA Big Book puts it, getting sober at 26 and picking up only one white chip. That's not nothing, considering that most of Jill Loree's childhood memories are infused with her father's drinking. Her mother, on the other hand, had a controlling, co-dependent streak that wouldn't end. Sounds dreary, right?

In this spiritual memoir however, Jill Loree artfully lifts the story out of the ditch and finds the grace weaving between the lines. *Walker* also merges in a touch of poetry—her own, her sons' and even her Dad's—adding heart, depth and levity to the telling. Her gentle wit and brisk writing pace keeps things moving along. True to the title, there's no need to stew in misery.

Today, Jill Loree's spiritual path is filled with the light of Christ, which is what she has discovered emerges from the core of one's being after clearing away the detritus accumulated in youth—just as the Pathwork Guide said it would. That's the deeper message she is now passionate about sharing, and which shines through in this warm telling of the story of her life.

Living Light

Living Light
On Seeking and Finding True Faith

What greater gift could we give ourselves than to wake up and bring forward the Christ consciousness that dwells within. To become a living light. Indeed, every time we listen for the truth, we will find the light of Christ within. And there is nothing greater for us to uncover than this, and to find true faith. For that's the moment we'll know there is truly nothing to fear.

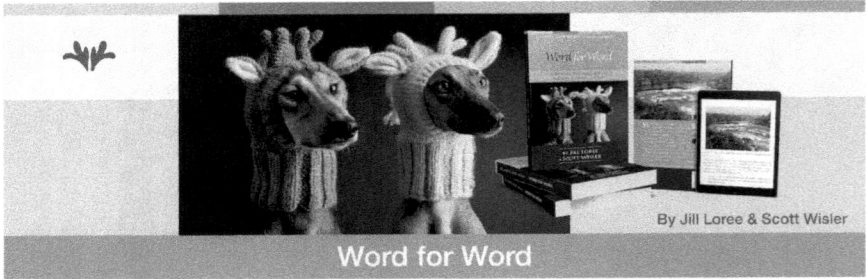

By Jill Loree & Scott Wisler

Word for Word

Word for Word
An Intimate Exchange Between
a Couple of Kindred Souls

By Jill Loree
and Scott Wisler

What does it really look like, not just to talk the talk, but also to walk the walk of a spiritual path?

Surprisingly insightful and at times pretty funny, *Word for Word* is a unique collection of text and email messages written back and forth between a couple of died-in-the-wool spiritual seekers, Jill and Scott, as they walked headlong into a new relationship that would prove lasting.

Typos and punctuation have been cleaned up to aid readability, but believe it or not, nothing has been added or subtracted nor has anything been tweaked so the two don't look too strange. You'll see.

Questions & Answers with the Pathwork® Guide

The Guide Speaks
The Complete Q&A Collection

By Eva Pierrakos
with Jill Loree

On *The Guide Speaks,* Jill Loree opens up this fascinating collection of thousands of Q&As answered by the Pathwork Guide, all arranged alphabetically by topic. This website includes hard-hitting questions asked about fears, hate, anger, health, relationships and so much more.

Jill Loree has combined her favorite questions about religion, Jesus Christ, the Bible, reincarnation, the Spirit World, death, prayer and meditation, and God into a single "Best Of" collection. You can read this collection online or download *Keywords: Answers to Key Questions Asked of the Pathwork® Guide.*

"There are so many questions you need to ask, personal and general ones. In the end they become one and the same. The lectures I am called upon to deliver are also answers to unspoken questions, questions that arise out of your inner yearning, searching, and desires to know and to be in truth. They arise out of your willingness to find divine reality, whether this attitude exists on the conscious or unconscious level.

But there are other questions that need to be asked deliberately on the active, outer, conscious level in order to fulfill the law. For only when you knock can the door be opened; only when you ask can you be given. This is a law."

    – The Pathwork Guide in Q&A #250

www.theguidespeaks.com

www.ingramcontent.com/pod-product-compliance
Lightning Source LLC
Chambersburg PA
CBHW060018050426
42448CB00012B/2803